The Olmec Civilization

An Enthralling Overview of the History of the Olmecs; Starting from Agriculture in Mesoamerica to the Fall of La Venta

Free limited time bonus

Stop for a moment. We have a free bonus set up for you. The problem is this: we forget 90% of everything that we read after 7 days. Crazy fact, right? Here's the solution: we've created a printable, 1-page pdf summary for this book that you're reading now. All you have to do to get your free pdf summary is to go to the following website: **https://livetolearn.lpages.co/enthrallinghistory/**

Once you do, it will be intuitive. Enjoy, and thank you!

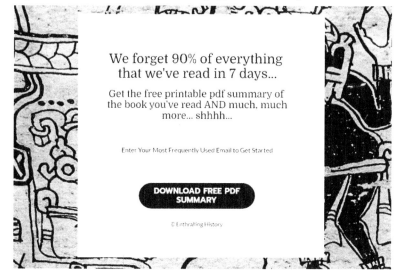

Contents

Introduction

Several civilizations have been described as shrouded in mystery due to inaccurate detailed information available to history lovers. The Olmecs civilization happens to be one of such civilizations with many unanswered questions.

The Olmecs arrived on the Gulf of Mexico around 1500 BCE and came with new engineering, religion, and agricultural ideas. Within a short while, they rose to the limelight and became the envy of the region due to their rapid development. There are questions like where they came from, their origin, and ultimately, what led to their fall?

Scholars are divided in their opinion about the Olmec civilization and the stories around them. Some historians opine that the Olmecs have origins from the region itself and are not migrants – as they have often been portrayed. In contrast, others believe that the Olmecs were travelers who settled in Mesoamerican and improved civilization.

In this book, we will be telling it all, and what better way is there to approach the topic than to begin with the Pre-Olmec Mesoamerican period where it all started? We have left no stone unturned on covering this topic. Also covered in this book are the Archaic periods and the different phases within the Mesoamerican region.

This book presents the Olmecs' amazing history and contributions to the modern-day regions in the most comprehensive and easy-to-understand way – more so than anything similar you might find. The author has consciously considered the concerns of beginners and those who struggle with history. Furthermore, the book will transit to covering everything you need to know about the Olmecs, from the origin to the fall. So, even if you struggled to understand history before now, you will have fun reading this one and recommending it to your friends and family.

Let's get right into it.

Chapter 1 - The First Settlements

The Archaic Period, which is the era that preceded the invention of pottery, is also known as the *preceramic period*. It is a period in Mesoamerican history that started sometime around 8,000 BCE (Before the Common Era) to 2000 BCE. This period was mostly known for the transition from reliance on mostly hunting for feeding to a more settled way of living which led to the rise of agriculture for feeding the fast-growing population. Mesoamerica is made up of modern-day:

- Costa Rica
- Central Mexico
- El Salvador
- Nicaragua
- Guatemala
- Belize

This Archaic Period is traditionally categorized into Early, 2000 to 1000 BCE; Middle, which was between 1000 to 400 BCE; and Late/Terminal Period, which was between 100 to 250 BCE. This period was before the Lithic (or Paleoindian) Period and followed by the Pre-Classic Period. It is still unclear when exactly the Lithic Period ended and when the Archaic Period started; however, many believe it was related to climate change – the metamorphosis from the ice age to the present – and the fact that remains from extinct animals from the ice age were never found.

The Archaic Period

This period was a notable time in the Mesoamerican regions because it marked the beginning of a change in lifestyle from people who moved about hunting for wild animals to more settled arrangements. With this emerging lifestyle, the people stayed longer in some of these places and, in the process, developed agricultural skills because they relied more on the produce than hunting. The first permanent settlements discovered were in the Gulf of Mexico, the Caribbean, and the Pacific Seacoast. These settlements are, for the most part as a result of the abundance of marine life and food resources.

Archaeologists discovered the use of various locations for different durations of time. For example, several sites on the Chiapas coast, like the Cerro de las Conchas, showed evidence of all-year settlements. Others can be found in modern-day Belize along the Caribbean coast, some inland settlements towards Cobweb Swamp and Colha.

Although the exact origin of Mesoamerican agriculture remains unclear, historians and scholars believe that several generations of people into major regions localized many species of wild plants during the Archaic era; these later served as the agricultural foundation of the Pre-Classic and Classic Mesoamerican civilization. These plants include beans, chili peppers, and maize, often grown together in a maize field.

While the origin of maize remains inconclusive and the debates continue, the regions that did well in agriculture – especially the domestication of wild plants – were the highlands of Oaxaca and Tehuacan, that is modern-day southeast of the Valley of Mexico, the coastal lowlands of the Gulf of Mexico and Pacific.

The more the people chose to stay longer in a particular place, the faster their populations increased due to the reliance on agriculture and other types of food found on the seashore. This population expansion soon led to the birth of a more sophisticated society differentiated mainly by their craft, trades, and emerging social class. These early Olmecs traded obsidian, chert, flint, textiles, and feathers.

Let's look at the categories that emerged during the Archaic Period, the difference in economic, cultural, and political developments. Also, we will be looking at the similarities and regional variations. Four primary Mesoamerican cultures emerged in the Pre-classic Period: The Valley of Oaxaca, the Olmecs, the Gulf of Mexico Littoral, the Valley of Mexico, and the Maya Zone.

Early Pre-Classic Period - 2000 to 1000 BCE

The central feature of the early Pre-Classic Period was the expansion in population and further complexity of the settlement. Some of the most notable advances found in archeological records include the creation of specialized crafts, unique figurines, and pottery. Also, during this period, there was more extensive trading between the regional networks, more social complexities, and the emergence of warfare.

Evidence of war within the region was discovered dating to 1800 BCE, especially on the Oaxacan valley among the Zapotec and other surrounding areas. These battles grew increasingly complex as the Pre-Classic period faded away and birthed the dominance of the Monte Albans over Oaxaca.

During this time, signs of widening social differences prevailed, including acquiring status goods, variation in the houses built, and funerary rituals. This period was also known for discovering the first form of ceramics in Mesoamerica around the Chiapas coast, extending to what is now known as El Salvador.

This early Pre-Classic Period also saw the emergence of the Olmec, the "mother culture" of Mesoamerican polities and states that followed.

Middle Pre-Classic - 1000 to 400 BCE

The middle Pre-Classic Period saw further development and expansion of these complex societies from the Early Pre-Classic. For example, unity and hierarchical government systems became widespread in the region like the Maya lowlands and highlands, Chalcatzingo, the Mexican Valley, and the Valley of Oaxaca. Some of these societies changed from traditional chiefdom systems to *states*.

This was also a time when kings and other royals were treated as the mouthpiece of the gods; hence they could not be questioned or opposed. This change in the approach to rulers was noted among the Monte Alban I of c. 500 – 200 BCE in the Valley of Oaxaca. During this period, the kings/rulers were *divinely selected*, so they answered to no one. All their words and actions were believed to have come from the gods.

The Middle Pre-Classic Period also experienced growth and population density, which made social differentiation more pronounced. The gap between the elite and the commoners widened further. The ruling and religious elites acquired spiritual powers to stamp their authority.

As for culture, this was a time of crystallization of the pan-Mesoamerican culture zone. There was massive and ongoing buying and selling of goods and exchanging ideas across the regions; this included religious beliefs and sacred items. Other high valued items and precious stones like pearl oyster shells, pyrite, jade, quetzal feathers, and magnetite were also exchanged. An immense jump in buying and selling was also notably ongoing during this period, and architecture took a front seat to it all with the construction of unique architectural carved monuments; one of them was found on the Oaxaca valley, dating back to 1000 BCE.

Furthermore, the introduction of idol worship started in 500 BCE. Among the Monte Alban 1 rulers, more than 300 idols were erected, carved with various inscriptions like dates and events. Many of these inscriptions included writings describing wars and the sacrifice of prisoners of war. Scholars are still studying some of these symbols.

The Maya, too, experienced some of these developments in symbols and monuments with massively carved stones or wooden slabs that displayed the ruler's power, authority, and legitimacy. The Maya monuments of the Pre-Classic period were carved from Chiapas to far as East and South El Salvador.

The need to take over and rule over other smaller areas increased considerably in the region. The population explosion helped intensify agricultural processes, and we see the development of more complex water control technologies. The increased complexity of the society was also felt and seen in the pottery designs as production soared and became available in more sophisticated and elaborate forms.

Later/Terminal Pre-Classic Period - 100 to 250 BCE

This period was defined by the veritable urban transformation, which laid the foundation for the flourishing presence of states and polities of the Classic period. For example, in the North and Western parts of the region specifically, Nayarit, Colima, and Jalisco, there was gradual urbanization, state-building construction, and significant architectural edifices but not on the scale seen in the other parts of the region. In the southern region, the Monte Alban II of c. 250 BCE to 1CE, the rulers held tight to power and control over the area while expanding the construction of residential and ceremonial centers. Construction of the colossal city of Teotihuacan began during this period. Located in central Mexico, this civilization would later dominate most of the Mesoamerican region.

The North and West, which is modern-day Nayarit, Jalisco, and Colima, experienced urbanization, state-building, and monumental architectural development but on a lower scale when compared to other regions. The style of pottery, artistic designs from these regions, and funeral rituals and practices further reflected the apparent regional variations among the territories.

In the Eastern part of Mesoamerica, there were massive developments of all kinds, notably in the Tres Zapotec of the Olmecs along the Gulf Coast. On the other hand, neighboring locations like La Venta and San Lorenzo declined in power and influence.

The Mayans stood out among the societies in the region that experienced rapid developments in the terminal Pre-Classic period. The people developed and advanced their writings, astrology, and mathematics. Their architectural skills were notable in their structural designs and urban planning. They also won and dominated more territories within the region, giving them more power and control.

Other advancements in this civilization eventually made them unique in the Classic period.

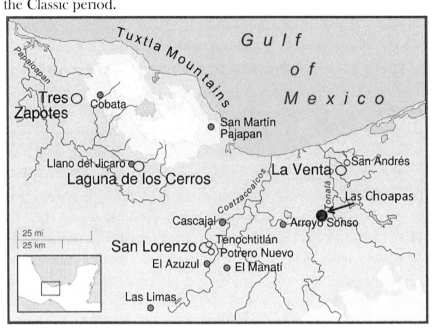

Olmec heartland

Early Settlements

The Archaic period was an era of transition for the Mesoamerican people who gradually transformed from being wondering hunter-gatherers to partly settled or sedentary rummagers and farmers. Based on a study's outcome on remains at the Mexican Gulf Coast, humans started co-existing and built permanent houses close to each other between around 3000 and 1800 BCE. They began with items that could get burnt easily and later to more durable material and structures. The people participated actively in trading activities, especially obsidian trade.

Examples of these early changes are temporary, seasonal shelters, like the Gulia Naquitz, a rock shelter in the Valley of Oaxaca. A band of nomads was discovered to have used this shelter as a settlement between 8000 and 6500 BCE at least six times. The speed of this development was not at the same rate in all the regions.

Also, travelers and temporary settlers took shelter in the El Gigante rock shelter located in the Southern Highlands of modern-day Honduras. Evidence that the rock shelter was only occupied during the wet season was supported by the presence of a unique type of plants, which could only have gotten there by settlers who used the place mainly during the wet season from July to September. Also, during the Archaic period of 4,700 BCE, from May to October. Several settlements that merged into a village-like arrangement were identified around the Chiapas sea coast and the Caribbean.

It was clear that the Sea and Lagoon nearby provided resources that made the settlers stay longer and, in most cases, all year-round. Shell mounds found at these sites were examples of evidence that proved this extended stay, and some of these shells have been dated back to between 5500 and 3500 BCE.

Additionally, the non-existence of Archaic animal remains, and the short supply of artifacts further revealed that Cerro de las Conchas was used more as a collection and processing point for sea and lagoon resources. While this site might have been temporally inhabited, the situation was different at the inland camps with signs of all-year-round settlements.

> "More permanent sites are identified in the archaeological record with greater frequency dating to 3000 BCE and later. The site of Zohapilco on Lake Chalco in the Basin of Mexico has evidence of year-round settlement before a volcanic eruption around 3000 BCE. The site of Colha and nearby swamps, such as Cobweb Swamp and Pulltrouser Swamp, show evidence of permanent settlement by 3000 BCE. Actun Halal, a rock shelter in Belize, was occupied as early as 2400 to 2130 BCE. Permanent villages are seen even later in the Valley of Oaxaca by 2000 BCE and in the Valley of Tehuacan by 1500 BCE. Based on these findings, it appears that people settled in resource-rich areas, such as

along the coasts or by lakes, earlier than in semi-arid and arid environments like the Valleys of Oaxaca and Tehuacan. As agriculture developed, the population increased and settlements expanded into more marginal, less resource-rich areas. "Extracted from Wikipedia - Mesoamerican Archaic Period.

Based on these discoveries, it appears that the resource-rich areas like the coasts by the lakes were first used as settlements and more heavily populated than the semi-arid and drylands, such as in the Valley of Oaxaca and Tehuacan. The more agriculture developed, the more populations expanded and more settlements we required; that led to the expansion into more minor resources-rich marginal areas.

The El Gigante Rock Shelter

At 1300 meters above sea levels and above the Estanzuela River Valley, the El Gigante rock shelter gives you a comprehensive view of the Southern part of today's Central Honduras. Only authorized personnel are allowed; the site is completely enclosed due to the lower rim being 3 to 4 meters above the slope leading to it. Over thousands of years, the presence of accumulated sediment at the entrance tells a story of how the vault shields settlers in the rock shelter from rain and wind.

These same conditions have made it possible for the settlers to survive through different seasons and remain consistent in the advancement of their vocations. Evidence of preserved vocations has been found among the artifacts recovered from the area, including leather and woven fibers remnants. Another significant find at the El Gigante is the region's most prominent and probably the most preserved basketry collection, dating to 11,000 years. That makes it one of the oldest artifacts found in Mesoamerica.

Also found in the El Gigante are human remains, showing that giant humans once took shelter in the rock. Additionally, there are many bones from sea species like crab, as well as deer, armadillos, and rabbits. Also discovered are plant remains like avocado, hog plums, wild beans, soursop, and most recently, cobs of early domesticated maize.

Mesoamerican has been described as one of the first places in the world where wild plant domestication occurred. The massive collection of well-preserved farm plants further buttresses the accuracy of the timing and trajectory of domestication in Central America and the Mesoamerican territories. Beans, maize, and squash were some of the plants well-preserved and discovered at this site. We also had a further understanding of how the settlers managed their prized trees through the presence of an extensive collection of partly-domesticated resources like coyol palms, ciruela, acorns, and several species of sapote. An even more profound understanding of this domestication was seen in the samples of avocado pits and rinds.

Based on the archeological test performed on botanical remains found in the rock shelter, the early human settlement at El Gigante dates back to about 11,000 years ago to the Archaic period. Between 5,700 and 2000 BCE saw the transition from a larger scale to more aggressive cultivation of maize – mainly because the original tropical forest retrogressed in the valleys nearby due to massive fires. These fires made the people move from their previously favored pine-oak lands, massively migrating from the original highland villages to lands where they could farm more around the valley floors.

El Gigante is not the only rock shelter in Honduras, but none of the others that come close to it are *deposits*. El Gigante is indeed massive and majestic, with its cubicle measured at 42 mm wide, 17 mm deep, and 12 mm high. Again, unlike what is obtainable at the other rock shelters around Honduras, only a few negative paintings of hands are left of the rock-art collection from El Gigante. Based on all discoveries to date, no other rock shelter comes close to El Gigante in size, dimension, and setting in all of Central and Mesoamerica.

Chapter 2 - Domesticated Agriculture

Adaptation of Agriculture

The domestication of agriculture refers to adapting or evolving wild plants into types that can be cultivated for or raised for human consumption – and this was the predominant type of farming in the Archaic period. However, it took the people of Mesoamerica thousands of years to adapt agriculture as a means of livelihood due to many reasons, but primarily due to rainfall, soil types, and the terrains. The increased dependence on the domesticated plant was a much slower process for the people of the region.

It appears that climate change impacted the resources available to roaming hunter-gatherers and led them to adopt new ways of getting food. No doubt climate change played a massive role in the emergence of plant domestication, but there are other complex reasons why people started depending on agriculture as their means of livelihood. While the Archaic people boosted their reliance on domesticated plants, they never stopped moving from one place to another in search of wild plants and hunting animals, which was their predominant means of feeding.

The first forms of cultivation (and the early stages of domestication) possibly involved some variation of dooryard horticulture. The Archaic people used some of the lands in their settlements or shelters to plant and nurture different plant species. Gradually, agriculture started booming along with the demand for domesticated crops. The Archaic people resorted to farming methods like the slash-and-burn due to the increased demand for more land for agriculture. With this method, they were able to recover more lands away from their settlements and villages.

Farm tools like the chipped stones adzes (a tool similar to an ax) give us a deeper insight into how digging took place and how trees were cut down to gain more ground for farming during the Archaic period. We also understand the people from this period better – and most significantly, how they interacted with the environment.

The people of this era preferred the farming method of slash-and-burn cultivation style. As the name suggested, it involved cutting forest trees to make room for more farmlands, as evidenced by the high level of charcoal found at the sites. The burnt layer of ash provided the freshly cleared land with rich nutrients to fertilize the crops. Other evidence that supported the use of slash-and-burn included the presence of low levels of pollen and the several corn pollens found at the site. This style of farming was used for farming several crops, especially maize dating 7300 BCE in the Caribbean and Balsas regions.

Between 5200 BCE and 3,500 BCE, we confirmed wide forest clearing in the Maya lowland on the Gulf coast. Additionally, charcoal levels at the Chiapas coast remained high after 3500 BCE, suggesting more people's attempts to recover more farmlands. The farmland recovery and high charcoal levels continued into 2500 BCE when the people started moving closer to sea and lagoon resources. This migration has been linked to forest clearing using the burning method. Paleoecologically, evidence across the north of Belize showed that people started cultivating manioc and maize before 3000 BCE. However, massive forest clearance and increased maize farming only began after 2000 BCE.

Towards the end of the Archaic period and into the Pre-Classic, the Mesoamericans started improvising on different types of farming, as discussed below.

Terracing

The terrace farming method is a set of sloped structured earth on the plane ground cut into consecutive declining flat platforms or surfaces. This farming method is labor-intensive and one of the earliest types of farming dating back to the Archaic period. The heap of earth looks like long stretches of steps, and they make farming more effective.

Graduated terraces are commonly used to cultivate on hilly surfaces or mountainous terrains. Also, they serve as a means of regulating erosion and surface runoff, and they are also used for growing crops that need irrigation.

Raised Fields

This type of farming is done on a large and elevated piece of land, bounded mainly by ditches filled with water to control environmental factors like frost damage, moisture level, and flooding. Raised field agriculture was primarily common among the pre-Hispanics in Latin America, like people from Budi Lake Mapuche and tropical lowlands.

These Pre-Hispanic raised fields are quite familiar from the regions near Santa Cruz de Mompox in the northern part of Colombia and the Llanos de Moxos region of lowland modern-day Bolivia. In the highlands of Bolivia, the Tiwanaku tribe close to Lake Titicaca also used this farming method, called "waru" or *camellones*. There are also ancient raised fields that have been traced back to Central America at Pulltrouser Swamp in Belize, where the Maya civilization practiced this type of farming. Other Ancient people who practiced raised fields were the people of Toltec and Aztec on the shore of Lake Texcoco, where it was called *chinampas*.

Crop Rotation

Crop rotation was another system of farming observed to have started in the Archaic period and become common among the Mesoamericans. The adaptation to these farming systems helps increase farming activities and reduces the over-reliance on the slash-and-burn farming system.

Domestication Agriculture

As the people of Mesoamerica became more settlers than foragers, they became more reliant on agriculture and some particular type of plants, making Mesoamerica one of the largest independent plant domestication areas in the world. The requirement for surviving the settlement arrangement included unique and intensive domestication processes, like selectively collecting bigger seeds to cultivate and preserve.

Several sites have been uncovered to help us understand how and when agriculture started in Mesoamerica, but many details were tampered with, impairing our ability to piece together an exact picture. For instance, the Guila Naquitz site in southern Mexico possesses rich evidence of the transition from hunting to farming and food production by the Mesoamericans. Strong evidence of the use of edible plants like wild beans and seeds from other grass that provided nutrients was found. Others include:

- Acorn (Quercus species)
- Prickly pear (Opuntia species)
- Pinon pine nut (Pinus edulis)
- mesquite seeds (Prosopis species)

We also have plants like:

- Squash (Cucurbita pepo)
- Maize (Zea mays)
- Beans (in the Phaseolus genus)
- Chili peppers (Capsicum genus)

The Mesoamerican Archaic people chose plants they could conveniently preserve with a genetic makeup that can be tampered with easily. Some of these plants include chili peppers (Capsicum genus), squash (Cucurbita pepo), beans (in the Phaseolus genus), and maize (Zea mays). The successful farming of these domesticated plants led to a boost in a more dependable food supply for the

Archaic peoples, making room for more settlements and population expansion.

Domestication of Maize

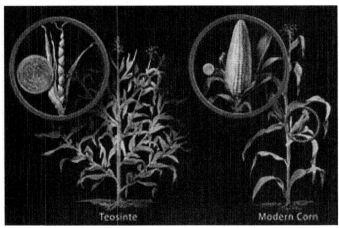

Maize was probably one of the most important crops to be domesticated during the Archaic period. It also played a critical role for the Mesoamericans because it was valuable, nutritional, and easy to preserve. Despite its popularity and use among the regions and in archaeological records of the Mesoamericans, the actual origin of corn is still shrouded in misery. While the oldest maize cob was discovered in cob form in Gulia Naquitz dating back to between 6,300 and 6000 BCE, it is most likely not domesticated there (because it showed up suddenly in a domesticated form).

One series showed that multiple mutations had been claimed to be responsible for the domestication of the maize cob; however, there are no records for these mutations. Instead of relying on conspiracy or guesswork, the researcher decided it was better to conduct genetic analysis. This approach eventually paid off because it showed a different wild plant, gamma (Tripsacum acetylides), was a wild plant crossed-bred with teosinte to produce the structure of the modern-day maize. Unlike teosinte, Tripsacum was entirely edible. The Mesoamericans possibly identified teosinte-Tripsacum in the wild and decided to cross them for trials. There's also the possibility of tests of the teosinte with other plants with sugary leaves and stalks.

Mesoamerican chewed leaves and stalks of early maize for the sweet flavor it provided. At the same time, starch and sugar were also valuable ingredients for producing alcohol, which was a vital consumable for social gatherings.

Archaeological evidence revealed that the Balsa region was one of the first sites where the corn was domesticated before spreading to the neighboring areas. Also, teosinte has been genetically traced to the wild plant domesticated as maize. Highland Mexico is one of the known locations where the earliest maize was sighted. After going through the process of radio carbonation, the two maize types (Zea diploperennis and Zea mays parviglumis) found at the Gulia rock dated back to 4300 BCE.

The maize found on the Chiapas coast around 3000 BCE could only have been a trade product because of the form in which it was found. So, it was not a surprise to find maize in neighboring Colha about the same 3000 BCE, which would have spread to Northern Belize within the same timeline. It was no longer new to find maize by 2600 BCE in Guatemala, Mirador, Nakbe, and Central Belize, specifically in Actun Halal by 2210 BCE.

Notwithstanding its origin and where it was first domesticated, maize became a staple crop in the Mesoamerican regions and various settlements. It was prepared and consumed in different forms: maizemeal paste, flat cake, tortillas, gruel, or even ground or boiled in limewater.

Domestication of Squash

The dates of remains found at the Gulia Naquitz sites suggest that the region's people carried out multiple squash domestications. A good example is a squash (Cucurbita pepo) which appears to have also been domesticated around 8000 BCE. Like the maze, squash was another widely domesticated plant and spread across the regions through trade. Various squash seeds bigger than the ones from the wild were also discovered at the Gulia Naquitz site, further proving that domestication was taking place. One of the biggest of these squash seeds has been dated to 10,000 BCE, one of the oldest validations of domestication by the Mesoamericans.

Unsuccessful Domestication

It was clear not all the domestication attempts by the Mesoamericans were successful. They had several failed and abandoned attempts, like that of the wild plant *foxtail*. Additionally, the San Andres site is filled with evidence of abandoned domestication like the pollen from domesticated cords dating to 7000 to 6000 BCE.

Cotton seeds and pollen dating to 4000 BCE were also found at the site; researchers believe they came from domesticated wild sunflowers, but the people seem to have encountered some difficulties with the Mexican sunflower. It appears the wild plant which was found in eastern North America belonged to another species. The other reason for the problem could have been due to the mobile nature of the low-density population. The bottled gourd (Lagenaria siceraria) was the other domesticated non-edible plant domesticated around the same 8000 BCE found at the Gulia Naquitz site. However, the bottled gourd was non-consumable farm produce; instead, it was used for water and other liquids.

Leftovers of wild plants like a different version of squash, corn, manioc, chili pepper, and beans were discovered on tools dating to the Archaic period sites around northern Belize, which further clarifies that these plants were already domesticated since that period. About the same time, other essential crops were found in the region and included Cacao, cotton, quinoa (Chenopodium quinoa), common beans, lima beans, and tomatoes. In terms of domesticated animals, this period was found to have dogs, Muscovy duck, and turkey.

Villagers and Agriculture in Mesoamerica

The village settlements were still uncommon in Mesoamerica until the Early Formative Period, which started around 3800 BCE, after the domestication of maize. The village setting was formed by the parents and their children's family, the extended family. This extended family provided the workforce required to care for the farms. Steadily, small unit settlements became villages, and later – based on nearby flat-topped pyramids – larger local units flourished.

Eventually, societies believed to be more advanced, like the Olmecs, constructed large towns notable for molding colossal stone heads. By 2000 BCE, more refined and developed societies had emerged and dominated smaller formative groups like the Toltec, Maya, and Aztec. Technology was developed to supply water to all-year-round farming across all the smaller towns and empires. Food channels were also created to meet the need of urban centers.

Chapter 3 – Tools and Trade

The more Mesoamerican's moved away from roaming hunting as their primary feeding source, the more they embraced agriculture. As we have seen, the conversion of wild plants into edible ones spread across the regions, and more members of the population depended on agriculture. This dependence means more land will be needed for farming, which automatically means tools will be required to farm effectively.

The Northern Belize Chart-Bearing Zone (NBCBZ) seemed to be the hub of manufacturing stone tools in the archaic period. There was massive evidence of stone tool materials, technologies, and uses during this period. There was also much adaptation and diversification in using these tools around archaeological sites like the Colha. One of the most effective tools was the NBCNZ chert or the Colha chert, which was higher quality and different from the cherts made from other regions. By early 3000 BCE, the Colha chert had emerged as a primary material for forming stone tools. This evolution of stone tools did not stop, as it was also observed in the Pre-classic and Classic periods.

Another special-purpose production workshop was discovered within Colha, where constricted adzes (were manufactured in large quantities. This discovery suggests the origin of the commercialization of stone tools, especially as Constricted Adzes of the same style and shape were found in all the Mesoamerican regions. The tools manufactured were mostly bifacially constructed from local chert. For example, Constricted adzes were almost general-purpose tools used chiefly for digging, cutting woods, and clearing the forest for more farmlands.

Quite a number of stone flaked tools were found across the region, but the notable ones were the bifacially Lowe and Sawmill points. These tools were mainly used as fishing tools and weapons for hunting or even as knives. The people applied different methods in the filling of these tools to keep them sharp and effective. Practically all stone tool production methods practiced in subsequent periods were present and prevalent in the Archaic periods. Evidence of stone tools used in processing farm produce like cutting and grinding was found on chipped and ground stones.

More about these tools later; first, let us talk about trade.

Trading

Not much is known about trading in the Archaic period. There is evidence here and there showing that trading and long-distance buying and selling occurred during this period. On the other hand, stone tools were used to confirm the possibility of trading activities and networks in all the Mesoamerican regions. Some archaeologist has pointed to the fact that the coastal people of Chantuto in Southern Mexico bought and sold obsidian. For example, 57 high-value obsidians belonging to the highlands of Guatemala ended up at the Tlacuachero shell dump in Chiapas.

Their presence there could only have been through trading and also to be possibly used for trading. It was also discovered that settlements around the Basin of Mexico traded to buy foreign green obsidian instead of traveling to harvest it from the source. Furthermore, Colha Chert from the region has been discovered outside Mesoamerica, indicating that the Colha chert might have been involved in trade exchanges.

Tools

Now let's take a critical look at some of these tools that played vital roles in the transition from a foraging way of life to a more sedentary arrangement that involved farming. As we have seen earlier, some of these tools were also used as a product of exchange in trade, but were they also used as currency? We shall see.

Obsidian

Environmental examination of the origins of the obsidian was part of the research carried out in the region, which revealed how the precious rocky object was used in long-distance trades. It further provided details on the relevance of the obsidian in the daily life of the region's people, particularly in the performance of rituals, trade, and socio-cultural lives.

According to Wikipedia, "It is obtained by either **quarrying** source sites or in **nodule** form from riverbeds or fractured outcrops.

Following the removal of the **cortex** *(when applicable),* **bifacial, unifacial,** *and expedient* **flake stone tools** *could be produced through* **lithic reduction.** *The use of pecking, grinding, and carving techniques may also be employed to produce* **figurines,** *jewelry,* **eccentrics,** *or other types of objects.* **Prismatic blade** *production, a technique employing a* **pressure flaking**-*like technique that removed* *blades from a **polyhedral core**, was ubiquitous throughout Mesoamerica."*

Production Methods

The glassy internal structure of the obsidian makes it easier to structure into different edges. It tends to break in predictable and straightforward ways through the fracture in the rock. This contributed to its abundant use in the Mesoamerican regions. Obsidian is obtained in nodule form or through quarrying from fractured outcrops or riverbeds. Once the cortex is removed, where necessary, unifacial, bifacial, and proper flake stone tools can be made through lithic reduction. Other purposes of the obsidian include grinding, pecking, and carving techniques to produce eccentrics, jewelry, figurines, and other objects. Widely common among Mesoamerican people was Prismatic blade production, a method of applying pressure flaking that detaches blades from the polyhedral core.

Many regions in Mesoamerica did not have direct access to the obsidian source, which made distribution quite limited. This scarcity led to a different method of managing the tool to rejuvenate it—some of these methods involved re-sharpening the edges for grass cutting and other purposes. As the tool becomes blunt, the function is charged from cutting to other uses like scratching and scraping. Other forms of sharpening the precious rocky stone and extending it involve shaping it to look like other tools such as drills. They were also made to serve as projectile points.

Locations in Mesoamerica with Obsidian

As mentioned earlier, obsidian was not available in large deposits across the regions irrespective of its uses and popularity. Here are locations where archaeologists have confirmed the availability in great quantity.

In the South-central lowlands Gulf of Mexico

- Altontonga and Zaragoza
- Las Derrumbadas
- Pico de Orizaba

- Guadalupe

Central Lowlands of Mexico

  - Partodo
  - Cranzido

On the Highlands of Mexico

  - Santa Elena
  - Paredon

In Central Highlands of Mexico

  - Malpais
  - Otumba
  - Tapalcingo
  - Tulancingo
  - Zacaultipan
  - Multiple quarries in Pachuca

In West Mexico

  - Zinapecuaro
  - Ucareo

San Martin Jilotepeque, Tajumulo, Ixtepeque, Tajumulco and El Chaval are known sources and location where Pre-Colombians Mesoamericans exploited. It is also confirmed that nearly all the obsidian found in Maya and Olmec sites came from these locations.

Value or Worth

The relevance of obsidian in Mesoamerica can be compared to that of modern-day steel now. The rocky glass was massively distributed across the regions via trade activities. However, there is evidence of different values placed on obsidian by different regions within Mesoamerica. A good example is during the Pre-Classic period, obsidian was quite rare and only found mainly in the lowland regions with high status and ritual value.

Also, among the Mayans, evidence revealed the obsidian was primarily found among the privileged. The lower-class Mayans only started having access to more obsidian towards the end of the Classic period. Even then, the upper-class Maya people continued to access the limited supply of prestigious Teotihuacan green obsidian.

The value of the obsidian is slightly different among the Teotihuacan people, where the obsidian was traded as a waste of human effort in movements across long distances. The obsidian was exchanged or traded for high-status prestigious items. Teotihuacan is a rare type of obsidian that played an essential role in its rise to power and served as a trade element that boosted the growing economy.

Valuable items like ear-spools contained elements of obsidian. However, this item was also found among the lower-class people. So, the value placed on the obsidian varied. Obsidian was a vital trade item with different values, but there is no evidence that it played the role of a currency in Mesoamerica.

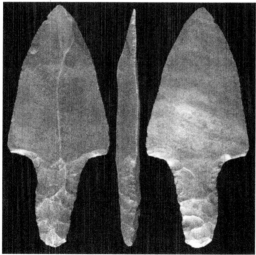

Colha Chert

Population expansion and the need for more arable lands are responsible for stone tool workshops at the Colha site. The high level of Cenozoic limestone present in Colha indicated how the site and the workshops made the most of the sources and location of the site. The people also developed a niche for themselves by using a well-traveled route to boost trade for their type of chert in the Maya trade market, which might have expanded to the Greater Antilles.

Colha was the primary supplier of chert within the region during the Pre-Classic and Classic periods. There were 36 workshops found at the Colha site. They were estimated to have produced well over four million cherts and obsidian tools and eccentrics distributed primarily through trades within the Mesoamerican regions during the Maya reign. This placed the chert on the same higher level of relevance as the obsidian.

Flaked Stones

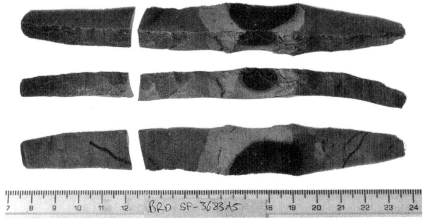

Flaked stone tools were essential in pre-Hispanic Mesoamerica and served many purposes, including ceremonial, militaristic, and domestic uses. The multicolored stone tool was found in what is known as present-day El Salvador, some parts of Honduras, Belize, Guatemala, and Mexico. Flaked stone is another product made from obsidian used for multiple activities. Flake tools are made in bifacial or unifacial forms to have projectile points like knives.

However, this equipment was not as standard as other blade tools aside during the early Mesoamerican prehistory or at a site like Colha where cherts were manufactured, and obsidian was in short supply.

Constricted Adzes

The constricted uniface, bifacial or chipped stone adze is a diagnostic tool discovered in the Preceramic period and northern Belize of Mesoamerica. Special-purpose workshops were also found in the Colha site, where constricted adzes were manufactured. This tool was primarily used for clearing the forest to create more land for farming. Additionally, it was known to be effective for digging and cutting wet and dry woods.

Lowe and Sawmill

Also discovered at the Colha site in Belize (and dated to the Archaic period between 8000 to 900 BCE) are 54 Lowe Points, 21 sawmill points, 4 Allspice, and 2 Ya'axche points. These bifacial stone tools are often diagonal on alternate-opposite edges and indicate various levels of reworking and re-sharpening, which impacts the size and shape of the blade and the size of the tool. The Lowe and sawmill served different purposes to the region's people; they have been used as spear points, harpoons, knives, and dart points.

The Lowe points, in particular, were affixed to thrusting or throwing spears. They have also been used as knives. On the other hand, Sawmill points were used as spear throwers, dart points, and knives.

Spears and Harpoons

In addition to farming, hunting and fishing were other vital means of livelihood for the people of Mesoamerica. The predominant tool used for hunting and fishing is spears and harpoons. Historically, Mesoamerica was the only Archaic civilization in the world that thrived without the successful domestication of animals like cattle, horses, sheep, and pigs. So, gathering, hunting, and fishing provided all the nutrients required by the growing population, which means the farmlands and the aquatic environment were the most productive landscape in Mesoamerica.

Spears and harpoons played vital roles in successful hunting and fishing in Mesoamerica. The harpoon is a long spear-like weapon used in fishing. The head is made up of carved stone, and in some cases obsidian, the edges are rough such that when it pierces the animal, the rough part of the weapon will pull it out of the water. The process involved thrusting the spear into the water quick enough to spear the fish and get it out of water. The harpoon was also used for hunting fast-moving marine mammals and large fishes.

Metallurgy in Mesoamerica

Metallurgy is extracting, purifying, and modifying metals and metal fashioning by people of the Americas before the Europeans arrived at the region in the late 15th century. A recent discovery showed that gold artifacts were found in the Andean region as far back as 2155 – 1936 BCE. In North America, copper dated to about 5000 BCE, which means the indigenous Americans have been familiar with and using metals from the Archaic period.

Also, these metals would have been discovered and used in their natural form without the need for smelting and shaping into desirable forms using hot and cold pounding and without the use of chemicals for modification and blending. There has not been any evidence showing this metal's melting, smelting, and casting in prehistoric Northern America. However, the story was different in the southern part of America. The people of the region did a lot of smelting and casting and deliberately mixed other metals.

For Mesoamerica, and Western Mexico in particular, Metallurgy noticeably developed after the contact with South Americans through marine traders from Ecuador and Colombia. Like in other parts of the Americas where the metals first appeared, they became material for the elite in the Mesoamerican region. The peculiar color, reflection, and quality appealed to the elite and led to several technological advancements within the region. Lookalike metal artifacts were found in Western Mexico and used in the same way the Ecuadorians used theirs. There were archaeological discoveries of items like needles, copper rings, and bells, which were cast using lost wax casting similar to those in Colombia.

Several other tools were discovered within the region during this period, but these are the most prominent ones. The process and method of making these tools include striking these stones directly against each other and hard and soft hammer flaking.

Chapter 4 – Important Sites and Artifacts

We now focus our attention on critical Archaic remains discovered as a result of extensive research. Several sites like the Valley of Oaxaca, home of the Zapotecs, the Tehuacan Valley, the location of the Cuscatlán Cave, Colha, Gulia Naquitz, and the Chiapas coast were explored, and many artifacts were discovered, which we will also be discussing – in no particular order.

Valley of Oaxaca

"Valles Centralles" or Central Valleys is the name it is fondly called today, but in the Mesoamerican era, it's mostly called Valley of

Oaxaca, and it is a rich site for many people in the region. Today, it's a state in southern Mexico and consists of districts like Ejutla, Tlacolula, Ocotlan, Zimatlan, Zachila, Centro, and Elta. The "Y" shaped valley is located within the Sierra Madre Mountains. The shape looks like a right side up alphabet "Y," with each point of the alphabet having specific names; the northwestern Elta arm, the central-southern Valle Grande, and the Tlacolula to the east.

This valley was also home to one of the most advanced societies in the region, the Zapotecs, and later the Mixtec culture, who dominated several smaller territories for a long time but later got run over by the Spanish. Like the Tehuacan Valley, Oaxaca has been inhabited for more than 10,000 years.

Several archaeological findings were made at the different sites in the Oaxacan valley, including findings at Geo-shin, Gulia Naquiltz, Monte Alban, Mitla, and San Jose Yagul. Oaxaca City, located at the heart of the valley, is currently the state capital.

Archaeologists discovered many historical sites in the Oaxaca Valley, including San Jose, Yagul, Monte Alban, Mitla, Gulia Naquitz, and Geo-shin. Currently, Oaxaca City, the state's capital, is located in the valley's heart.

Zapotec Civilization

The Zapotec people, also known as the "Cloud People," lived in the Southern highlands of central Mesoamerica in the Valley of Oaxaca. They occupied the land from 500 BCE to 900 CE, the latter Pre-Classic period to the end of the Classic. The initial capital was at Monte Alban and later Milta. Although they were notable for their advanced societies, had good dealings with others, and shared similar cultures with advanced civilizations like the Olmecs, Teotihuacan, and Mayan, the Zapotecs also oppressed the southern highlands with their advanced army and weapons. They were known for being good "businessmen" and even adopted their version of the Oto-Zapotecan language.

Origin and Advancement

The Zapotecs, like several societies in the region, emerged from the population that relied heavily on agriculture and expanded in the Oaxacan valley. They developed advanced methods of agriculture and stood toe to toe with similar civilizations in business dealings. For example, they had a grand alliance with the Olmecs on the Gulf Coast that furthered the construction of an impressive capital site at Monte Alban and stretched their oppression for the region during the Classic period. From the city's look, you could tell it was deliberately and strategically constructed to overlook three important valleys that developed between 500 BCE and 900 CE.

Zapotec consists of other vital settlements different from the capital, and more than 15 elite palaces were identified in the city's valleys. There are shreds of evidence that the Zapotecs might have been divided into three separate groups:

- The Valley Zapotecs, based in the Valley of Oaxaca
- The Sierra Zapotecs, in the northern part
- The Southern Zapotecs, based in the south and east around the Isthmus of Tehuantepec

The well-known Zapotec sites can be found spread across the "Y" shaped Valley of Oaxaca. They are Milta, Tlacolula, Abasolo, Ocotlan, Zimatlan, Zachila, San Jose Mogote, Etla, Huitzo, Oaxaca, and Monte Alban. Mitla would later place a significant role in the history of the Zapotecs. The city is notable from 900 CE for its unique buildings strategically arranged around plazas, richly decorated ornamented with reliefs and symmetrical designs.

As we draw a curtain on the Pre-Classic era, there were notable advancements in the unique type of art of the Zapotecs. They further improved in their writings and pushed further in architecture with unique designs and construction of centers for different gods and purposes. In engineering projects, they developed improvised irrigation systems among several cities within their control. For example, at Hierve el Agua, artificial terraced hillsides were constructed to transfer water from the canal of natural springs to several farmlands across the city.

The Zapotecs did not advance in isolation; they had contacts with other people within the region for different purposes. For instance, evidence at sites like Dainzu tells the story better. A large stoned-faced raised stage with reliefs reveals players playing a particular Mesoamerican ball game while wearing protective gear. It gets even more interesting because, in the basin of Mexico, the Teotihuacan's had an admirable relationship with the Zapotecs that they reserved a quarter of their cities for any Zapotecs willing to settle there.

Zapotec Writing

The Zapotec people developed a unique writing system known as one of the first in the Mesoamerican regions. Those that followed, like the Maya, Aztec, and Mixtec civilization, improved on it. They used a logo-syllabic system of writing that uses different symbols to represent each syllable of their language.

The Many Phases of Monte Alban

The story of Zapotec is incomplete without talking about the Monte Alban phases because that was where the formation took place. As mentioned earlier, some of the Monte Albans' noticeable advancements were unification and divine kingship. The unification of Monte Alban and Zapotec led to external domination and political expansion towards the end of Monte Alban 1 (400 BCE to 100 BCE) all through Monte Alban 2 (100 BCE to 200 CE).

Powered by a better and improvised military and weapons, Zapotec rulers from Monte Alban conquered and plundered kingdoms beyond the Valleys of Oaxaca. Their dominance was so compelling and pronounced that by the end of the second monte Alban, the Zapotecs' military and political dominance had spread from Quiotepec in Northern to Ocelotepec and Chiltepec in the South.

Monte Alban cities became famous and admired for their political, religious, and cultural influence in the region and retained this status until 700 CE.

Religions, Deities, and Artifacts

Like what we have in modern-day, the Zapotec religion was rich and confusing, just like several Mesoamerican religions. There were deities for things or events that appeared regular like Sun, Rain, Wind, Earth, and even War. Among the most important ones was the

Bat-god, the deity of fertility and corn

Beyda, the deity of wind and seed

Casino, the deity of rain and lightning

Patio Cozobi, a deity of corn

Copijcha, the deity of sun and war

Coquebila, the god of the center of the earth

Huechaara, a female mother goddess of hunting and fishing,

Kedo, god of justice,

Ndan, androgynous god of the oceans,

Pixee Pacala, the god of love

Coqui Xee, the god of infinity.

Also, individual cities and villages were known to have their guardian deities. For example;

• Coquenexo (Lord of Multiplication), guardian of Zoquiapa,

- Coqui Bezelo, and Xonaxi Quecuva (gods of the underworld and death), guardian of Milta and Teocuicuilco
- Cozicha Cozee, guardian of Ocelotepec.

The people offered prayers, offerings, and sacrifices to these deities in the hope of bringing good fortunes and intervening in their affairs. For instance, they prayed for crops to grow well, for rainfall to end a drought, or for the gods to bring fertility to the land and the populace. It was commonplace in the Mesoamerican region for the societies to use symbols to represent different days of the months; the Zapotecs adopted this. For example, Pija was represented by drought, Xoo, earthquake, while A crocodile represented chilla.

There are indications that the Zapotec carried out human sacrifices, especially to the fertility gods, and performed elaborate ritual ball games in the Monte Alban court. Also common were cleansing and dedication rituals for new religious sites and temples when completed. Also found were evidence of rare pieces of pearls, obsidian, and jade found in a stockpile in Oaxaca to support this claim.

The Fall of the Zapotecs

Although they tried to avoid confronting the Spanish invaders, the Zapotecs were eventually overrun and destroyed by the Spaniards after losing a war to the Aztecs from 1497 to 1502. The invaders took advantage of the weak military and peace-seeking of the Zapotecs and defeated them after five years of trying, which ended in 1527.

All attempts at revolting by the population were quelled by the arrival of steel weapons and new diseases. Later again, there were uprisings here and there against the new government and ruler, but they were all checked. However, hundreds of Zapotec dialects and seven languages survived and are spread all over Mexico and Los Angeles, California.

Tehuacan (tewa'kan) Valley

The Tehuacan Valley is located in the southeastern part of the Valley of Mexico and has been inhabited for more than 10,000 years. In 1960, the site was surveyed and excavated by archaeologist Robert MacNeish, and his team and the discoveries made have been very beneficial and key to understanding the people of Mesoamerica in the Archaic period. However, there have been controversies about some of the artifacts and other items found at the site, leading to multiple new analyses and examinations. In a particular site on the valley was the Coxcatlan Cave, which contained 15 to 33 components from the archaic period. Items found include;

- Small maize cobs,
- Remains from squash beans,
- Chili peppers and bottle gourd.

Modern-day Tehuacan, nicknamed "The Place of Gods," is the second-largest city in the Puebla, Mexico, in the southeast of the Valley of Tehuacan and surrounded by states like Veracruz and Oaxaca.

Maize Domestication

Historically, the Valley of Tehuacan was the first place archaeologists found the oldest farmed maize. From the exploration and findings on the site, archeologists believed the Valley of Tehuacan was the origin of the first maize cultivated by man. The discovery of more than 10,000 cobs of teosinte in the Coxcatlan Cave further buttresses their conclusion. Among the original findings in the cave were maize (only the size of a cigarette!) with not as many corn seeds as what we have today, wild and inedible maize, and teosinte.

Further re-evaluation was carried out on the findings at the site, and it involved testing samples from neighboring sites like Cueva Coxcatlan and Cueva San Marcos. The earliest dates were 4700 BP or 3600 BCE. Newer sites with evidence of early maize have been recently discovered in the Balsas River valley that continued downstream into the Guerrero state. More evidence has emerged that further confirms Balsas River Valley as one of the first sites in the world where teosinte was initially being cross-bred with other edible plants – more than 9,000 years ago – to produce the type of maize we have today. The peculiar teosinte from Balsas, which has now been confirmed as one of the first sources of domesticated maize, was mainly found at the valley's heart and was believed to have grown in other parts of the valley.

Coxcatlan Cave

Richard MacNeish and his team, while on an inspection tour of the Tehuacan Valley, discovered the Coxcatlan Cave in the Tehuacan Valley of Puebla Valley, Mexico. It is now a Mesoamerican archaeological site where more than 75% of stone tools were excavated.

There are several zones in the Coxcatlan Cave. To understand it better, archeologists have divided the zone occupied by humans into four cultural phases; the Ajuereado, El Reego, Abejas, and Coxcatlan phases. These phases were separated based on changes in stone technology, basketry, woven matting, and the pattern of settlements.

The zones inhabited by settlers who did not get involved in pottery, also known as the Preceramic zones, are the first levels of the rock shelter. The principal evidence of humans in the Tehuacan Valley happened during the Ajuereado phase.

The Coxcatlan phase dating between 5000 and 3000 BCE was when the settlers and inhabitants carried out a lot of cross-breeding between wild plants and edible ones. Discoveries also revealed that humans and animals shared time at the cave due to the non-permanent nature of the humans. These people were predominantly hunters, temporary settlers who constructed make-shift villages.

Artifacts

Some relevant artifacts found in the Coxcatlan cave dated to 5000 BCE. For example, the maize cobs, beans, and squash were some of the oldest versions in the region. Ink pen with vessels was another artifact found at the cave and discovered to use material traced to the Preceramic era.

Further analysis of the excavated items at the site revealed more information about 42 types of occupation by the people, 28 dwelling places, and seven cultural phases. Other archaeological zones in the Coxcatlan Cave uncovered signs of the ceramic period type of occupation. At the same time, evidence supports the presence of archaeological remains in the top layers of the cave.

Colha

The Colha archaeological site is another critical location that unveils a lot and plays a crucial role in the Mesoamerican period. It holds a rich history of workshops, stone tools, and the equipment used to transition from hunting to farming by people of the region. Located in the northern part of the country, Colha, Belize, is a Maya archaeological site. It is one of the earlier sites in the Maya region of Mesoamerica. It continues to hold relevant archaeological records of the Maya people and culture deep into the Pre-Classic period.

Excavation from the archaeological site in Colha made it easier to describe the occupation of the people from Early Preceramic 3400 - 1900 BCE to the Middle Postclassic period of 1150 – 1300. Its population expansion peaked in the Late Pre-Classic 400 BCE-CE 100) and in the Late Classic CE 600 – 850. These peaks in population expansion had a lot to do with stone tool workshops at the Colha site.

Colha was reputed as the access to top quality chart due to its strategic location around well-traveled routes in the region. It was also located around a principal source of Cenozoic limestone. The Mayans took advantage of these and created a niche for themselves as the source of the best chert in the region. This market later extended to the Greater Anthills. Colha eventually became the leading supplier of stone tools for the whole Mesoamerica from the Pre-Classic and Classic periods.

Figures obtained from Wikimili suggest that *"an estimated 4 million obsidian, chert tools and other important tools were produced and distributed in the Maya era and they all came from the 36 workshops located at the site."* So, when it comes to the trade and distribution of tools and rare items in Mesoamerica, the story is not complete without the mention of Colha and the Mayans.

The Presence of Obsidian at the Colha Site

In addition to the numerous workshops for constructing and carving stone tools used for hunting and farming, there was evidence of the high presence of top-quality obsidian at the Colha archaeological site.

According to a 2017 Cambridge University Publication,

"This study explores the early use of obsidian at the Maya site of Colha in northern Belize and the implications that variations in source distribution have for the site and its regional connections. Energy dispersive x-ray fluorescence (EDXRF) analysis of 104 specimens of obsidian from Preclassic contexts at the site identified El Chayal obsidian as the most common overall followed closely by that from San Martin Jilotepeque. Ixtepeque obsidian, not common in many Preclassic assemblages, was also strongly represented. The results revealed a Middle Preclassic dependence on San Martin obsidian gradually diminishing through the Preclassic to the Classic period, when San Martin all but disappears from the site. A corresponding increase in El Chayal obsidian use through time at Colha coincides with the rise of Kaminaljuyu in the Guatemalan highlands. Analysis of the obsidian by context indicated that El Chayal obsidian dominated in architectural and ritual deposits while Ixtepeque obsidian was the most common in workshops. San Martin accounted for a slightly greater percentage than El Chayal obsidian in middens, with Ixtepeque materials notably less common. The data indicate that Colha was connected to a broad distribution network from the Middle Preclassic onward, and that obsidian source variability was greater during the Preclassic than the subsequent Classic period."

(Brown, D., Dreiss, M., & Hughes, R. (2004). Preclassic Obsidian Procurement and Utilization at the Maya Site of Colha, Belize. Latin American Antiquity, 15(2), 222-240. doi:10.2307/4141555)

Gulia Naquitz

The Gulia Naquitz Cave in Oaxaca, Mexico, is an archaeological site notable for the early domestication of several crops like squash from Cucurbita, bottled gourds (Lagenaria siceraria) teosinte, the wild ancestors of maize. As far as the continent was concerned, Gulia Naquitz was the site of the earliest known domestication of squash. Although there was evidence backing the presence of maize in its early wild form, a closer reexamination of the pollen and the location of the find proved that the maize could not have been domesticated there. It is likely a product of trade or some form of exchange.

Way of Life

Although evidence revealed the earliest human presence dates to about 10,750 BCE, settlements did not continue all year round. For example, humans stopped inhabiting the rock shelter about 500 BCE. Evidence revealed how the rock shelters inhabitants were not permanent settlers; instead, they were preceramic hunter-gatherers who inhabited the rock shelter on six different occasions, mainly around August to December.

Domestication

The earliest indication of squash domestication dates back to 8,000 – 10,750, which was 4000 years before the domestication of other crops like beans and maize in the region. Evidence to support this was found during the 1960 excavation of the cave and four other Mexican caves.

Further exploration was carried out at the Gulia Naquitz site in 1970 by a team from the University of Michigan, which provided more accurate dates to support evidence of domesticated C. Pepo (field pumpkin) in the form of increased skin thickness and larger trunks in the newer level layers of the cave. By approximately 8000 BP (Before Present Years—the term is mainly used in the field of geology and archaeology with 1950 as the starting year), the field pumpkin trunks found were more than 0.39 in (10 mm) thick. Wild Cucurbita stems were below the 0.33 In (10 mm) limit. These changes in fruits' size and shape are signs of intentional cross-breeding of C. pepo, which occurred not later than 8000 years BP. About the same time, the average skin thickness increased from 0.033 in (0.84 mm) to 0.045 in (1.15 mm).

The agricultural technique of domesticating wild forest crops occurred more than 5000 to 6,400 years in Mesoamerica, starting with squash, then followed closely with the maize and then the beans, making them a part of the three sisters agricultural system of companion planting. Other edible plants recovered at the Gulia Naquitz site include pinyon, acorns, hackberries, cactus fruits, chili pepper, Amaranth, Chenopodium, agave, and mesquite pods.

Chiapas Coast

Chiapas de Corzo, is home to the Pre-Columbian Mesoamerican archaeological site in Chiapas. The site has been occupied since the Early Formative period of ca. 1200 BCE. It became famous as the regional center around 700 to 500 BCE during the Middle Formative period. By this time, its public territory had reached 18 to 20 hectares in size and settlements close to 70 hectares. Chiapas controlled the routes due to its proximity to the Grijalva River, located in the Central Depression of Chiapas. The hills and courts at the site date back to 700 BCE, with palaces and temples built towards the end of the Formative or Pre-Classic period between 100 BCE and 200 CE.

Artifacts and Important Findings

Archaeologists' fundamental discoveries include the 2008 finds of a considerable Middle Formative period Olmec ax deposit at the lower part of Chiapas de Corzo's Hill eleven pyramid. This Olmec ax deposit date back to 700 BCE and is the second of this type of findings in Chiapas after the neighboring San Isidro.

The oldest pyramidal tomb in Mesoamerica was discovered in 2010 when archaeologists found a 2,700 years-old tomb of a dignitary inside Hill 11. According to Bruce Backhand, the tomb looked more like an Olmec dignitary than a Mayan.

Also found at the Chiapas site is the oldest long count calendar discovered in Mesoamerica, December 36 BCE, found on Stela 2. All that is left of the ruins is the day-name and digits "7.16.3.2.13.).

Chiapas is also known for its broken pieces of ceramic materials containing Epi-Olmec script dating to as early as 300 BCE. These pieces are the oldest examples of writing yet to be found.

This unique archaeological site contains possibly the first examples of a palace complex built on hills in Mesoamerica. The royal tower, which was ceremoniously taken down some centuries later, was elegantly constructed in the first century CE.

Mesoamerica was rich in clay products, but none comes close to what was found in Chiapas, especially in the formative periods where clay artifacts like cylinder seals and flat clay stamps were found. Also, in terms of burial arrangements and cemetery organization, Chiapas showcased the most comprehensive and probably the best ordered and subdivided in the whole region as far as the formative period was concerned. More than 250 burial places have been dug up at the famous Chiapas de Corzo site, dating to the formative period. Quite a number of these cemeteries were located below hill 1 plaza.

In the whole Mesoamerican region, there's no site where more ceramic artifacts in the form of flat stamps and cylinder seals were found like those found in Chiapas. For example, Tlatilco Hieroglyphs were discovered at the site suspected to have been carved around 100 BCE.

Gheo-Shih

This area is nearly two hectares of open land located on the Milta River delta below the Gulia Naquitz site. This site was mainly occupied during the Middle Archaic period of 5000 to 4000 BCE and was famous for some unique artifacts found there like:

- Ground-stone tools
- Butchering tools
- Projectile points

- Drilled stone pendants

Other exciting discoveries at this site were rocky structures that were possibly used as shelters, an arrangement of stones that formed what looked like a court, a dance arena, and a road.

Santa Marta Cave

This archaeological site is located in highland Chiapas, Mexico, and was temporarily inhabited by hunter-gatherers till 3500 BCE and later dumped until 1300 BCE when farmers occupied it again. Items found on the site are teosinte cocoa pollen and ground-stone tools.

Zohalpico

This site is at the edge of Chalco Lake in the Valley of Mexico. The people were year-round inhabitants who depended on farming and agriculture for sustainability. There was evidence that they might have domesticated Amaranth and corn during this time.

te was later covered and taken over by ashes from a volcanic eruption which made it inhabitable for a long time. However, it was once again occupied within the next century. After the eruption, there was multiplication in maize pollen, pumpkin, and gourds.

Actun Halal

It was strategically sited in Macal River Valley in Western Belize. The rock shelter was occupied around 2,400 to 1210 BCE, and some of the artifacts found there include signs of production of cotton, Constricted adzes, and Maize.

Xihuatoxtla Rock Shelter

This site is located at the creek of the central Balsas River and dates between 6990 and 6610. Hand and milling stones and 251 chipped stones were among the items discovered at the site.

Tlacuachero Shell Mound

This archaeological site was one of those that settlers in the regions used seasonally. The primary activities at this site are processing marine resources like clams, fish, and sea turtles. The discovery of 57 obsidian flakes suggests they were products of trades or exchanges with other societies within the region. Also excavated at the site were two tombs.

Cerro de las Conchas

We have talked about several shell mounds; the list is incomplete without the one found at Cerro de las Conchas dating between 5500 and 3500 BCE and measuring close to 4 meters high and 100 meters wide. This was another seasonal site used primarily for marine transactions. The site is located at the edge of El Hueyate Mangrove harbor.

Chapter 5 - The Origin of the Olmecs

The Olmec – General Overview

The Olmec are fascinating people with a great culture. The whole Mesoamerican region had a unique civilization and advancement that raised questions about who they were, if they were initially from Mesoamerica or if they were travelers. We are going to unpack all of that and more in this chapter.

Archeologists and explorers believed the Olmec culture and civilization existed long before the Mayan or Monte Albans, and they go way back to 1800 BCE. There is even evidence to support their existence long before that time in places like modern-day Guatemala. The Olmecs have been appropriately identified as the first temple builders in all of Mesoamerican and what is known as Mexico and environs today, and it's definitely not the Mayans.

Several advancements that were previously credited to the Mayans have since been traced to the Olmecs. For example, the famous long-count Mayan Calendar (and others found in the Maya era) originated and was developed by the Olmecs. Some of the reasons why the origin of the Olmecs is shrouded in a lot of controversies include the clues of some epic Olmec scripts that suggest the emergence or combination of multiple cultures that form the civilization.

Some theories support the fact that the script was from Africa; others have argued that they may be Chinese, and another group concluded they might be Polynesians. All the arguments are familiar: the Olmecs did not look like native Mexicans or even Native Americans. A little more on these controversies later.

All the attributes ascribed to the Olmecs, like the level of their civilization, the uniqueness of their cultures, and how different they were from the other people in the region, are known as "archaeological civilizations." That means, based on a collection of artifacts that archaeologists thought to belong to a particular society. In essence, archaeological cultures are based on the generic appellation of the objects discovered in that areas and not on text.

In this instance, scholars concluded that all the artifacts excavated in the area covering the northern Isthmus of Tehuantepec dating from 1200 - 500 CE could only have belonged to one culture and civilization known as the Olmecs. For example, the name *Olmec* (which means "rubber people" or "rubber producers") was not particularly the name of the people, but a scholar put it together. He derived the name from a combination of Aztec (Nahuatl) words "Olmecatl." The words "people who dwell in the rubber nation." So, people just simplified it to rubber people. This is mainly because Olmec references the place where most of the artifacts were found and the production of rubber that went on there.

The Olmec site is a major center of activities, with several cities emerging and known for different historical purposes. Still, none is as crucial to the story of the Olmec civilization as La Venta and San Lorenzo. Modern-day Veracruz is about 35 miles on the southern part of the Gulf of Mexico and stood tall and popular around 1150 - 900 CE. Similarly, La Venta, which is Modern-day Tabasco, was located about 9 miles on the eastern part of San Lorenzo around the Mexican Gulf Coast. On its part, La Venta reached its peak around 900 to 500 CE.

Discoveries at the locations where the Olmecs dwelled revealed further information about the people and the type of diet they relied on. For example, food items like maize and other crops were not originally from the people. Instead, they were added because they predominantly relied on fishing and hunting for their diet and livelihood.

The Olmec people were credited for being skilled at creating massive structures like the many colossal stones heads found at the sites. Some of the other creations on that list include massive stone thrones used by rulers to depict power and divinity and different type of slaps that serve multiple purposes. They undoubtedly created the popular ball game, which was quite common in all the civilizations within the region. Part of the evidence that supports this is that the object of the game, the ball, is made of rubber, and the Olmecs were the people close to the source of rubber, and they were pretty good with creating items from the raw material.

The Olmecs were good with their production of rubber items and creating structures out of the soil. They built sand structures like pyramids, ceramics, and mounds of different sizes and shapes until they were predominantly known for their unique significant size creation. Their unique structures also influenced several civilizations in the region.

The Olmec civilization was one of the most robust and advanced cultures that influenced the early Americas. Although in the last century we started to see their strong influence dissipate, especially with the arrival of the Common Era, the Olmec civilization is still referred to as the mother culture of other societies that showed up in the regions many years down the line.

There were well-known cultures like the Teotihuacan, Totonac, Maya, and Zapotec civilizations famous for their unique arts, outstanding architectures, and advanced cultures that put them ahead of the other cultures in the Mesoamerican region. However, all these civilizations still have their origin traced back to what they shared with the Olmecs at some point in time through contacts.

The Origin of the Olmecs

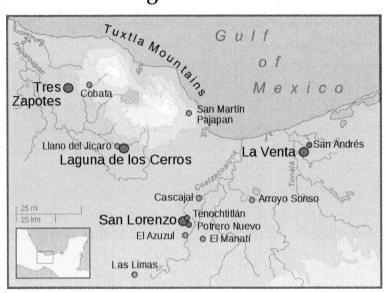

As mentioned earlier, the people of the rubber nation, also known as the Olmecs, were the most influential and stood out during the Mesoamerican era. All other known civilizations can trace their advancement to the Olmecs. As a result of the rapid developments the people experienced in Soconnusco, they settled in today's Veracruz and Tabasco, or what is known as the hot and humid valleys of Mexico.

The origin of the Olmecs is shrouded in deep controversy, and we will look at some of these controversies later and what led to the conclusion by these scholars involved. One account believed that the Olmecs possibly came from neighboring Mixe Zoque or Mokaya civilization.

The formative period primarily belonged to the Olmecs because they thrived and expanded extensively in the Mesoamerican region around 1500 to 400 BCE. The Olmec era is divided into two; the Pre-Olmec cultures mainly existed from 2500 BCE, but by 1600 to 1500 BCE, the Early-Olmec culture had commenced and was located in San Lorenzo Tenochtitlan on the southeastern coast of Veracruz.

From their various practices and ways of life, it was accessible to how they laid a solid foundation for other emerging civilizations in the region to copy, adapt and make improvements. It was also clear that the Olmecs practice blood-shedding rituals; whether it was a human sacrifice or animal sacrifices, the controversy is still on.

Some scholars have put the commencement of the Olmec civilization at 1400 and 1200 BCE; however, some later excavations and discoveries have since adjusted the origin to 1600 – 1500 BCE. These discoveries were at the shrine in El Manati, San Lorenzo. Eventually, the Olmecs adopted the diets available in the region, like farming maize and other food crops. There were signs of farming being a major source of livelihood from some of the remains discovered at Tabasco and further suggested that they likely started around 5100 and 4600 BCE. These diets and food items were also adopted by later Olmec civilizations just as they did the technologies.

The development of the Olmec people and their culture was made easy by the ecosystem, consisting of well-watered alluvial soil. In addition to that, the Coatzacoalcos river basin provided the people with a great transport network. There has been a strong comparison of the Olmec environment and climate with other advanced civilizations like the Nile, Indus, and Mesopotamia.

The productive nature of the environment ushered in a good and bad experience for the people because the dense population started giving rise to classes. Eventually, the elite class emerged and pushed for the production of unique items to differentiate the Olmec culture. This would lead to producing some of the known luxury artifacts, symbols, and sophisticated items.

Several of these luxury items made from magnetite, jade, and obsidian were out of the reach of the lower class of the population. They were items for the rich, and the fact that they came from outside the Olmec society does buttress the point that the people had extensive trading activities within the region. There are three likely sources named as the origin for the high valued obsidian found among the Olmec elites. For example, the most luxurious jade found among the Olmec elites has been traced and found to have originated from the eastern part of Guatemala, known as the Montague River valley. It could have come from El Chayal, which is closer to the Olmec society in the highlands of Guatemala. Other likely sources are Puebla and San Martin Jilotepeque. These locations were only some kilometers away from the Olmecs.

A few sites shed more light on the Olmec culture due to some Olmec artifacts found there. One such site is the Mezcala culture which is in modern-day Guerrero. There was more Olmecs type of artifacts found there than those found in the Veracruz – Tabasco sites. A city known as Teopantecuanitlan in Guerrero is one of such cities relevant to the Olmec culture. One other relevant object from the Amuco-Abelimo site, an apparent Olmec creation that dates back to 1530 BCE, was found in Guerrero.

The Colossal Heads and The First Excavation

The colossal heads have turned out to be synonymous with the Olmec civilization. They molded human heads from massive stones or large pieces of movable rocks. They are of different heights from 3.8 to 11.2 ft. some of these heads have been found to date back to 900 BCE. The question has been asked what these heads genuinely represent or if they were worshiped as gods or if they were a representation of some royalties. It would seem more like the latter dues to the different features on the faces.

Most of the heads were that of matured adults with the following features:

- Fleshy cheeks
- Slightly-crossed eyes
- Flat noses
- headdresses
- Frowning or smiling faces

- The back of the stones is often flat with no unique designs since they are not meant to be seen as much as the front.

To further bolster this point, these features are still found among the locals of modern-day Veracruz and Tabasco. From the remains found at the sites, it appears the carvings took place at the Sierra de Los Tuxtlas mountains in Veracruz and then moved to other locations within the civilization.

The massive size of the stone heads and the carving location revealed that the final products might have been transported either through a chain of humans or some means of transportation. The distance covered in moving these stones is sometimes up to 250 km. All these efforts put into the sculpting and movements of the stones further suggest their relevance to the people. The heads either represent some powerful leaders or some influential elites in the societies.

The efforts that go into each head almost made them uniquely different and evidenced that they were carved after particular individuals and not just a general production. Some of the heads were even carved wearing headgears, suggesting a representation of royalty or warriors. In the whole region, the Olmec colossal heads stand out and are unique to that civilization.

Jose Maria Melgar Serrano discovered the first colossal stone head officially in 1862. However, due to poor data collection and management, the discovery was not recognized or reported outside the shores of Mexico. Fast forward to 1938; the same site was excavated by Matthew Stirling, which led to the Olmec civilization's archaeological study.

Within the Olmec region on the Gulf Coast of Mexico, there were 17 stones heads found from four sites. Generally, most heads were carved from slightly rounded rocks or stones; however, two unique designs were found in San Lorenzo Tenochtitlan carved from giant stone thrones. Another structure was found in a nearby site in Guatemala, specifically at Takalik Abaj. It was a stone throne that looked like it was carved out of a colossal head. Also, it was the only structure that was found outside the Olmec society.

Arriving at an actual date for each of the monuments remains a major challenge for researchers and archaeologists because many of them were tampered with before the commencement of archaeological investigations. However, several of these Colossal Heads have been dated back to the Early Pre-Classic period of 1500 – 100- BCE, while a few others to the Middle Pre-Classics of 1000 – 400 BCE. The least colossal head weighs around 6 tons, while the bigger ones vary between 40 and 50 tons. It is important to note that the enormous, colossal head found seemed to be uncompleted and abandoned close to where the stone originated. The reasons remain unclear.

Fringe Theories of Alternative Origins

As mentioned earlier, the origin of the Olmecs seems to still generate quite a controversy among scholars, researchers, and archaeologists. Some suggestions contradict the generally known and accepted origins of the Olmec civilization and attribute it to have originated from other cultures, with Africa at the top of that list. Those who push these theories claim that contact with another world outside the Mesoamerican region might have led to the origin of the Olmecs.

While these ideas of other origins have been famous, they are still not accepted as the official position of mainstream researchers who are well versed in the region's history. Although these theories are considered fringe, the history of the Olmec civilization will not be incomplete without talking about them.

African Origins

Several scholars have been pushing the idea that the Olmecs originated from or were related to people from some part of Africa. These experts have based their theories on their personal opinion about the interpretations of some of the features of the Olmec artifacts. They further believed that the manner of speaking, way of life, genetics, general mannerism, and the structure of the bones found at the sites looked like those from some part of Africa.

The first person to push the idea of the African connection of the Olmec is the scholar who discovered the first colossal head in 1862 at Tres Zapotes (formerly Hueyapan), Jose Melgar. In the published paper, he likened the colossal head to that of a "Negro race." The opening in the publication was later proved in the early part of the 20th century by Leo Wiener and a couple of other scholars. Some modern-era supporters of this idea, like Clyde Admad Winters and Ivan Van Sertima, have further narrowed down the origin of the Olmec to the Mende people in the western part of Africa.

Suggestions of Epigraphic Proofs

These researchers and scholars mentioned earlier, along with other modern-day proponents of the idea that the Olmecs' origin came from Africa, claimed that the writing systems found in Mesoamerica, which we have traced to the Olmec civilization, look very much like the African scripts. Here's how some pushed their claims;

- Early in the 19th century, French Polymath Constantine Samuel Rafinesque opined that the popular Maya writing style and inscriptions could only have come from the Libyco-Berber style, which has its roots in West Africa.

- A linguist and an American historian, Leo Wiener (and a few others) thought that Epi-Olmec and Olmec symbols and Vai script share close similarities. The Vai script is from Liberia in West Africa. Other close similarities include:
  - ➢ Inscriptions on the Tuxtla Statuette,
  - ➢ Cascajal Block
  - ➢ Teo Mask
  - ➢ The Celts in offering at La Venta

Mesoamerican scholars and researchers have continuously debunked these claims of African origin or relation with the Olmecs. Great work is ongoing to translate the Maya scripts found at the sites, but the same cannot be said of the Olmec glyphs.

Chinese Origins

Similar to theories like African origin, some writers believe that Chinese refugees immensely impacted the Olmec civilization. They linked this influence to the ending part of the Chang dynasty. Here are some of those views and how they arrived at their conclusions:

> • Betty Meggers projected that the Chinese Shang empire played an essential role in the emergence of the Olmec civilization around 1200 BCE. She was of the Smithsonian Institution and an archeologist who was famous for her work in South America.
>
> • In collaboration with Chen Hanping, Mike Xu suggested in his book, published in 1996, that the La Venta celts thought to bear African marks originated from the Chinese.

Again, like the African claims, the Mesoamerican researchers have knocked down Betty and Mike's claims. According to them, Mike Xu's evidence could only have been coincidental markings and more look-alike than actual Chinese markings. They further pointed out that the Olmecs ceramics bore similar marking with the Chinese oracle bone inscriptions, but they are not related. In a 1997 article, Claire Liu extensively discussed the existence of jade in both culture and shared knowledge of the North.

Jaredite Origins

"In the Book of Mormon (1830), a text regarded as scripture by churches and members of the Latter Day Saint movement, the Jaredites are described in the Book of Ether as a people who left the Old World in ancient times and founded a civilization in the Americas. Mainstream American history and literature specialists place the academic setting for the Book of Mormon among the "mound-builders" of North America. The work is therefore classified in the American "mound-builder" genre of the 19th century.

However, Mormon *scholars and authors seek to demonstrate that events described in the Book of Mormon have a literal foundation. A famous* Book of Mormon geography model *places the scene of the Jaredite arrival and subsequent development in lands around the* Isthmus of Tehuantepec *in Mesoamerica. However, the tradition leading to this Mesoamerican model does not originate with the Book of Mormon, but with an enthusiastic interest in* John Lloyd Stephens's *1841 bestseller, Incidents of travel in Central America Chiapas, and Yucatan.* Mormon founder Joseph Smith *placed the arrival of the Jaredites in "the lake country of America" (region of* Lake Ontario*), allowing for the eventual migration of Book of Mormon peoples to Mexico and Central America."*

Therefore, some Mormon scholars identify the Olmec civilization with the Jaredites, citing similarities and noting that the period the Olmecs flourished and later declined corresponds roughly with the Jaredite civilization timeline."—extracted from Wikipedia.

Nordic Origins

On his part, Michael Coe wrote,

> *"The presence of Uncle Sam inspired Thor Heyerdahl, the Norwegian explorer and author of Kon Tiki, among others to claim a Nordic ancestry for at least some of the Olmec leadership... [However], it is extremely misleading to use the testimony of artistic representations to prove ethnic theories. The Olmec were American Indians, not Negroes (as Melgar had thought) or Nordic supermen."*

Michael Coe was an explorer and a cultural diffusionist.

The major takeaway from all the theories and counter-theory is that the Olmecs were a unique set of people who were possibly from more than one place. They were probably travelers who eventually settled in Mesoamerica because they showcased a peculiar civilization that originated from their society and later rubbed off on the whole Mesoamerican region.

While scholars have argued back and forth about the origin of the Olmecs, there has not been any form of an argument about the influence of the Olmecs on the region. Every known civilization in writing, technology, structures, monument, sports, and others in the region have been successfully traced back to the Olmecs.

Chapter 6 - San Lorenzo Tenochtitlan

General Overview

San Lorenzo is not merely another archaeological site in Mesoamerica. It has been confirmed as the oldest Olmec city established. Based on excavations at the city, there is evidence that the city had taken the form of an Olmec site as far back as 1150 BCE and was possibly invaded and destroyed around 900 BCE.

At a time when most Mesoamerican cities were outdated and without a form, San Lorenzo was already known for great advancement and achieving incredible feats, especially in the Early Formative period. Experts have attributed these exceptional developments and achievements to the peculiar location of the city and the ecosystem.

Not only did the city enjoy almost all year-round rainfall, but it also enjoyed rich seaside soil positioned along the broad. That is not all; it had rich artificial mounds that held water around the southern Gulf coast, which was great for their agriculture. This condition was perfect for maize farming, and it gave the Olmecs a significant edge over the rest of the regions. It was eventually known as the fertile crescent of the area.

However, as the population expanded, it became evident that the levee lands were not enough, leading to competition among the people for who would control what portion. The competition eventually led to rivalry and conflicts. Soon classes emerged and possibly led to the emergence and dominance of a powerful farming class who were possibly well-armed than the other members of the society. This incident would later lead to creating the elite class in San Lorenzo within the Olmec civilization.

In describing the physical appearance of the city,

> "In appearance, the San Lorenzo site is a compact plateau rising about 160 feet (about 49 meters) above the surrounding plains. Cutting into it are deep ravines that were once thought to be natural but are now known to be artificial, formed by the construction of long ridges that jut out from the plateau on the northwest, west, and south sides. Excavations have proved that at least the top 25 to 35 feet (about 8 to 11 meters) of the site was built by human labor. There are about 200 small mounds on the site's surface, each of which once supported a dwelling house of pole and thatch, which indicates that it was both a ceremonial center with political and religious functions and a minuscule town." Description extracted from Britannica.com

The Olmecs are fondly known for their advanced civilization and the numerous stone heads that littered their society and environs, but no other place compared to San Lorenzo in the carving, molding, and construction of stone heads. The site had unique stone monuments that were believed to have been images of powerful characters within the society. However, it was observed that several of these stone monuments were intentionally damaged at around 900 BCE. Many were buried in ridges and other locations. There were attempts to cart away some of these monuments, but the size and weight might have made it impossible to move, but smaller ones would have been taken away possibly by invaders.

Some of these monuments mainly were made from basalt and weighed as much as 44 tons. The basalt source was at the Tuxtla Mountains in Cerro Cintepec, where there was a volcanic flow. One mystery that still surrounds these stones is how they were moved to several locations with this community. Some theory talks about how the stones must have been pulled or rolled to the nearest stream and then mounted on rafts up the Coatzacoalcos River.

Another theory opined about how moving these stones to their desired location would have taken many days. One thing is evident in all of these theories, the number of humans that would have been needed to move these stone monuments would have been enormous, and the people responsible for moving the stones must have belonged to a lower class.

The stone heads are attention-grabbing due to the almost flawless look they have natural human faces. You can easily interpret the emotions expressed by each stone head from pain to power, control, and smiles. Most of these stone heads came from San Lorenzo. More about the stone heads later...

In addition to their advanced civilization and stone heads, the Olmecs were also known for their temples and deities, often combined with animals and humans. For instance, there's a popular deity of a partly jaguar and a human infant. Some of these deities were sculpted, entangled, or crying. Also, scholars have concluded that the "jaguar" is a central part of the Olmec art because it is often fused humans to form a deity. It also shed more light on the most recent nature of the Olmec society.

Olmec monuments and artifacts were primarily spherical, with a showcase of great technicality and skills. The striking resemblances would make you assume modern tools were used for these carvings, but in fact, stone tools were the main instruments used to achieve these remarkable feats. The methods used were pounding and pecking. Also noticeable is a unique design seen in the pottery and ceramic figurines that mainly were nude and without sex and had traits of the jaguar.

The presence of some exotic raw material in San Lorenzo showed the distinction in classes, and the taste for luxury items and further suggested the Olmecs were involved in massive trade networks within the region. Top on the list of the commodities traded was Obsidian which served as flakes, blades, and darts. These were mainly imported from Guatemala and the highlands of Mexico. Other luxury items traded for and found in San Lorenzo include:

- Iron ores, used as mirrors and other purposes
- Serpentine, used by goldsmiths

However, the jade was conspicuously absent in the region during this period and would not show up until after 900 BCE during the city's fall.

Further evidence of trading with the region's people was seen in the early Formative period when the Olmec sent out a small group from the Gulf coast into the highland of Mesoamerica in what seems like a negotiation for the safe passage of goods bound for San Lorenzo. Also, there have been discoveries of San Lorenzo type of ceramics in the form of figurines at various burial sites in the Valley of Mexico like the Tlapacoya and Morelos. The Olmecs continued to be actively involved in the region even into the Middle Formative period – and possibly at its peak.

San Lorenzo-type Olmec ceramics and figurines have been found in burials at several sites in the Valley of Mexico, such as Tlapacoya, and in the state of Morelos. There is evidence that the Olmec sent groups from their Gulf coast "heartland" into the Mesoamerican highlands toward the end of the Early Formative, in all likelihood to guarantee that goods bound for San Lorenzo would reach their destination. The Olmec involvement with the rest of Mesoamerica continued into the Middle Formative and probably reached its peak at that time.

Suffice to say; other known Olmec cities came to light in the Early Formative period:

- Laguna de Los Cerro in Veracruz, specifically the southern part of Cerro Cintepec, seems to have been another Olmec site because of their large number of unique sculptures found at the site.

- On the eastern part of the Tabasco border, La Venta was another known site that seemed to have only emerged after the peak and fall of San Lorenzo.

Now, let's get into details and specifics.

Why is San Lorenzo Relevant to the Olmec Civilization?

San Lorenzo is the name adopted by archaeologists to describe the location of three archeological sites, namely:

- The San Lorenzo site
- The Tenochtitlan site
- The Potrero Nuevo site

All three sites are located in Veracruz, Mexico. These sites alongside Tres Zapotes and La Venta were quite prominent and played pivotal roles in the cultural development and civilization of the Olmecs. By 900 BCE, San Lorenzo had established itself as the center of the Olmecs. These days San Lorenzo is known chiefly for the Olmec stone heads found there –especially one that weighs 28 metric tons and is about 9.8 ft high.

The San Lorenzo Tenochtitlan site can easily be mixed up with the Aztec site in Mexico, but they are not the same. The similarity is only in names, which was also due to some administrative translation of the Aztec words.

The Description of San Lorenzo

Artifacts dating to 1600 BCE found at El Manati were some of the earlier signs of the Olmec cultures. It tells how the previous settlers had taken to agriculture and lived in the site for hundreds of years before development came and eventually emerged into a regional center for the Olmec civilization.

The emergence of a complex state was first noticed among the Olmecs before other parts of the region eventually copied it. San Lorenzo was the first city to demonstrate such complexity. The site is responsible for dominating the gulf coast lowlands and imposing the

Olmec way of life on other territories. One of the colossal heads found at San Lorenzo stands at about 9.3 feet tall and 6.9 feet wide!

Mesoamerican researchers and scholars are unified in the division of the Olmec history to be broken down into four stages:

- The Formative - 1700 to 1300 BCE
- The Integration - 1300 to 00 BCE
- Expansion - 900 to 300 BCE, and
- Disintegration - 300 to 200 BCE

Another phrase commonly used by archeologists to describe the Olmecs time is the "Formative Period." This was the critical time when the state-like complexities started rising and gaining fruition.

Before its fall and the eventual emergence of the La Venta, by 1200 BCE, San Lorenzo was already the largest city in Mesoamerica, and it had that status up until 900 BCE. However, by 800 BCE, the human population at San Lorenzo had reduced to almost zero. Furthermore, there were attempts to annex the site's plateau around 600 to 400 BCE and from circa 800 to 1000 CE.

Unlike what was obtainable at La Venta, which was located and surrounded by a swampy environment, San Lorenzo was strategically situated in an ecosystem that was friendly for farming. The site enjoyed all-year rainfall, and the land was excellent for agriculture. Furthermore, it appears as though the place was more of a ceremonial city; even today, people from the Olmec society gather for rituals and events.

The city had no walls, and the people were, for the most part, medium to large scale farmers. It has been estimated that the San Lorenzo structures and ceremonial centers could accommodate 5,500 people and that the whole area along with the hinterlands could reach 13,000 people. These numbers are by far lower than the population that existed in the city back in its heyday.

There was evidence to support the conquering and dominance of neighboring territories. For example, San Lorenzo controlled a large portion of the Coatzacoalcos and its lands – even to the east, where La

Venta eventually emerged and became popular. Other areas like the Tuxtla Mountains had societies that were not under the control of san Lorenzo.

"Built on some 700 hectares (1,700 acres) of high ground between then-active tributaries, the core of San Lorenzo covers 55 hectares (140 acres) that were further modified through extensive filling and leveling; by one estimate 500,000 to 2,000,000 cubic meters (18,000,000 to 71,000,000 cu ft) of earthen fill were needed, moved by the basket load. The rulers of San Lorenzo played a crucial role in integrating a population that changed the natural environment into sacred and secular landscapes for the glorification of the San Lorenzo polity."

"Archaeologists Michael Coe and Richard Diehl calculated that the 77 square kilometers (30 sq mi) area of San Lorenzo that they studied could produce approximately 500 metric tons (490 long tons; 550 short tons) of maize annually, enough to feed 5,556 people, more than the estimated population at the time. Residents of San Lorenzo also consumed domestic dog, snook, tarpon, mojarra, catfish, and turtles. Although some claim that manioc was cultivated here, no evidence for this has been found." Excerpts from Wikipedia on San Lorenzo Tenochtitlan.

San Lorenzo was also known for its extensive and elaborate drainage system, which had been discovered to serve other purposes beyond providing water for the people. Scholars have linked the water supply system as worship to a supernatural water deity.

The drainages were uniquely designed and constructed using buried stones to form pipes that channeled water around. However, while fresh spring water was present at the elevated lands, the lowlands cannot be said. Again, this may be due to the existence of classes in the city among the people. For example, "U" shaped stones were arranged to control water to the edges of the high grounds, which is a clear sign of the ruling class displaying their control of the resources meant for the whole populace.

Initial Excavation and Archaeological History

Many research and archeological works have been carried out at the San Lorenzo site; it's also essential to add that there has been quite a bit of controversy. However, Matthew Stirling is recognized as the first person to start excavation in 1938 after several visits. Four other archaeological works were carried out on the site between 1940 and 1979, one of which was led by Michael Coe and Richard Diehl of Yale University between 1966 and 1968 (before taking a break and resuming in 1990.) Coe's work focused more on emphasizing the formation of patterns within the community and at regional levels among the Olmecs.

The name "San Lorenzo Tenochtitlan" was the brainchild of Matthew Stirling, who named the area based on the three nearby villages and settlements. All three locations were found around the west of Coatzacoalcos. The original name for the area remains unknown. On the other hand, Tenochtitlan's archeological site still bears the same name and falls within a village with the same name on the northern side of the Island, while Potrero Nuevo can be found on the hilly eastern part of the plateau.

Stone Sculptures of San Lorenzo

The San Lorenzo archaeological site is also peculiar for the types, quantity, and variations of sculptures it showcased. The expertise that went into some carvings is close to what we have in the modern era, but the sculptors mainly relied on stone tools to charge those astonishing results. Some carvings were for humans but of higher classes, while others represented the deities the people worshiped. As of the last count, more than 124 stone sculptures have been discovered, and it is believed that there are still a lot more buried and yet to be unearthed.

These stone images vary in size, from the massive Colossal Heads that weigh about 28 tons (because they were made from basalts which are bi-products of volcanic eruption and mostly found at the Cerro Cintepec) to smaller images the size of pots. The level of work on these stones only shows the power of a powerful character and a deity that the people worshipped.

The Eight Major Phases of Occupation

In their 1960 excavation exercise at the San Lorenzo site, Michael Coe and his colleague Richard Diehl listed the eight phases of occupation as follows

- The Orochi Phase, ca 1750 to 1150 BCE
- The Bajio Phase, ca 1550 to 1450 BCE. These two were the pre-Olmec Formative successions.
- The Chicharras Phase, ca 1450 to 1400 BCE. This was the period when more artifacts showed up at the site. It also falls under the Early Formative period.
- The San Lorenzo Phase, ca 1400 to 1000 BCE. The city reached its peak but later suffered a decline as we entered the Middle Formative period.
- The Namaste Phase, ca 1000 to 800 BCE.
- The Palangana Phase, ca 300 to 50 BCE. These phases saw a decline in population as we slid into the Late Formative period.
- The Remplas Phase, ca 300 to 50 BCE. There was no occupation record during this period like we had in the Early and Middle Classic periods.
- The Villa Alta Phase, 800 to 1000 BCE. Again, we saw signs of reoccupation of the site.

Architecture

Remains found at the San Lorenzo site suggest that the city might have been a hub for carving several sculptures found in the Olmec civilization. In addition to the sizeable colossal stone heads, giant thrones, felines, figurines, birds, images of more miniature humans, among others, were also discovered. Some of these images were symbols of the supernatural powers of the rulers and deities, while others represented some monsters. A significant percentage of these images were carved out of basalt brought into San Lorenzo.

One can quickly identify the classes in San Lorenzo based on their taste and the type of structures they lived in, even in the part of the city they chose to reside in. For example, the elites built for themselves large structures lifted on low soil platforms and showed their powers and authorities through some of the monuments found on the site. A particular elite structure named the "Red Palace" was constructed using compressed soil for the floors and walls and then plastered with sand mixed with hematite.

"Massive columns that were 4 meters (13 ft) tall and carved out of basalt supported the structure's roof, and L-shaped basalt benches are thought to have been used as step coverings. Blocks of bentonite clay and limestone have been found in the debris and may have been used in the walls. Several structures had walls that were made of thick mud and 40 centimeters (16 in) thick and lacked post-molds. They were evidently constructed using a rammed earth technique." *"Other structures employed bentonite masonry fixed with mud mortar. Floors were made of gravel or packed earth or paved with bentonite blocks."* Description was extracted from Wikipedia.

The lower-class people lived literarily on the lower part of the plateau, which goes down 40 meters below the higher lands. Their house was built with inexpensive materials like thatched wattle-and-daub.

The Olmecs displayed their technical skills in construction with the building of the San Lorenzo terraces. You could tell the amount of labor that had gone into creating such masterpieces. For example, one of the terraces hung from a 7-meter-high wall. It remains unclear if this was contracted at the order of their rulers or if it was an act of ingenuity by the lower-class people.

Carl Wendt, an Olmec Household archeologist, carried out further archaeological work in some areas in San Lorenzo to determine how the people lived and the type of structure they built. His study focused more on particular areas and not the entire site. For example, he studied the El Bajio part of Remilino and other central parts of San Lorenzo. Additionally, he paid special attention to the refuse and waste left behind to arrive at his conclusions.

Part of Wendt's findings included the fact that the architectural patterns and organization of the San Lorenzo lowlands were similar to that found in the Maya highlands houses and huts. The structures were replete in spaces and built to have different areas for separate activities like resting, cooking, storage and others. They further explained that although detached, they were structured to be a part of a central patio.

Exchange from San Lorenzo to the Rest of the Region

San Lorenzo was indeed the center of the Olmec civilization while it existed. Many artifacts like figurines and pottery designs were found all over the region. A good example was at the Canton Corralito archeological site in Chiapas, where more than 5,000 figurines, pottery works, and other objects that originated from San Lorenzo were found.

As a matter of fact, there were even more Initial Olmec objects (dating to 1250 – 1150 BCE) and Early Olmec objects (from 1150 – 1000 BCE) found at the same site – even more than found in San Lorenzo when they originated from. During the early Olmec period:

- 15% of the carved pottery is known as Calzadas Carved. They are believed to contain possible supernatural elements.

- 9% of the Incised pottery, known as Limon Incised, is primarily used for decorations in homes and temples.

All originated from San Lorenzo. Interestingly, no items found and examined in San Lorenzo originated from other parts of the region.

Chapter 7 - Cultural Achievements and San Lorenzo's Decline

Jose Maria Melgar was the first archeologist to discover the first Olmec stone head back in 1862 and wrote this about his findings,

> *"In 1862, I was in the region of San Andres Tuxtla, a town in the state of Veracruz, Mexico. During my excursions, I learned that a Colossal Head had been unearthed a few years before, in the following manner. Some one-and-a-half leagues from a sugar-cane hacienda, on the western slopes of the Sierra of San Martín, a laborer of the hacienda, while cutting the forest for his field, discovered on the surface of the ground what looked like the bottom of a great iron kettle turned upside down. He notified the owner of the hacienda, who ordered its excavation. And in the place of the kettle was discovered the abovementioned head. It was left in the excavation as one would not think to move it, being of granite and measuring two yards in height with corresponding proportions... On my arrival at the hacienda, I asked the owner of the property where the head was discovered, to take me to look at it. We went, and I was struck with surprise: as a work of art, it is without exaggeration a magnificent sculpture...what astonished me was the Ethiopic type*

represented. I reflected that there had undoubtedly been Negroes in this country, and that this had been in the first epoch of the world."

Since that time, more than 17 confirmed colossal stone heads had been found within the Olmec archeological civilization, and ten of those were discovered in San Lorenzo. We will focus more on the stone heads in this part since we have already discussed how the carvings were created, the likely means of movement, and the magnificent work in them.

The Ten Colossal Stone Heads of San Lorenzo

The colossal heads found in San Lorenzo seemed to have been arranged or placed side by side along almost equal distances from the north to the southern part of the site. A few stone heads were also found in ditches close to the sources but buried by erosion. This is contrary to some suggestions that they were hidden away from human sight.

It would seem as these heads formed some route that led to the central part of the city and possibly a showcase of power and authority of the traditional rulers at the time. Some stone heads have clearly gone through recarving, converting them from old thrones to serve other purposes. Here's a list of all ten stones and the information available about them. The colossal stone heads have been labeled numerically for easy identification.

San Lorenzo Monument 1 – Colossal Head 1

- Discovery: This particular colossal stone head was found facing up like someone asleep facing upwards. Erosion had created a path through the top of the head, which made it visible to the archeologist, who noticed the eyes and later other parts of the head. It was discovered in 1945 by Stirling and his colleagues.

- Size: it weighs about 25.3 tons, measures 2.11m/6.9 ft, wide and 2.84m/9.3ft high.

- Materials: Large quantity of broken ceramic were found around the stone alongside figurines

- Dating: Some of these materials have been tested and found to date back to 800 – 400 BCE and others as far back as the Villa Alta Phase of 800 – 1000 CE.

- Description: This stone was uniquely carved, showing a headdress tied by a headband to the back, probably to keep the hair from being rough from the wind. The upper part of the headdress is designed with decorations in repeated patterns to form a U-shape. The expression on the face is that of a wrinkled, aged character, with lips slightly open but still covering the teeth. His cheeks are puffy, and the ears were perfectly designed to reflect a unique deformation on that part of the character's face – or it could be a mistake by the sculptor!

• Current Location: Colossal Stone Head 1 is currently sitting in Museo de Antropologia de Xalapa.

San Lorenzo Monument 2 – Colossal Head 2

• Discovery: Discovered by Stirling in 1945, like the stone head 1, it was found face up facing the sky. However, this one was not an original because it was clearly undergoing a recarving process from a stone throne to a colossal head. You can tell from the apparent damage or incomplete nature of the alteration.

- Size: This stone weighs about 20 tons, stands at 2.69m/8.8ft high, and measures 1.83m/6ft wide by 1.05m/3.4ft deep.

- Material/Dating: The material found around this head has been dated to the Early Pre-Classic and Later Classic periods.

- Description: This monument was carved wearing a complicated headdress with a headband tied to the back of the head and three birds in the form of the character's forehead. Stone Head 2 was severely damaged from multiple holes appearing on the face and indicating abandonment, maybe because the reworking was not going well. However, from what we can see, the image seems to represent an elderly male character wearing a frown face with his lips slightly open to reveal part of his teeth.

- Current Location: Colossal Stone Head 2 is currently in the Museo Nacional de Antropologia as part of the exhibitions that tell the story of the Olmecs.

San Lorenzo Monument 3 – Colossal Head 3

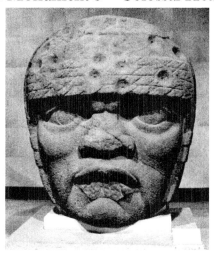

- Discovery: this stone head was discovered in 1946 by Stirling. Unlike stone heads 1 and 2, stone head 3 was found in a gully, face-down, and the wet ground made it particularly difficult to turn over and move. The actual origin of this stone head remains unknown, but it was found southwest of San Lorenzo.

• Size: This stone weighs 9.4 tons, measuring 1.78 meters/5.8ft high, 1.63 meters/5.3ft wide, and 0.95 meters/3.1ft deep.

• Description: This particular stone head has a frowning eyebrow with defined eyelids, thick, slightly parted lips, with a broken lower lip.

• Current Location: The stone head 3 is currently at the Museo Antropologia de Xalapa.

San Lorenzo Monument 4 – Colossal Head 4

• Discovery: Again, this stone head was discovered by Matthew Stirling in 1946. Stone head 4 seems to have been well-preserved when excavated, and it was found lying sideways. The head was found around the northwest of the central hill, towards the brink of the gully.

- Size: Stone heads 4 weigh only 6 tons, 1.78meters/5.8ft high, 1.17 meters/3.8meters wide, 0.95 meters/3.1ft deep.

- Material: The ceramics material found at the location of stone head 4 was consistent with that found at the site of stone head 5, making it difficult to arrive at an accurate date.

- Description: The face is nicely structured to look like an elderly male with lower cheekbones, a creased forehead, and a slightly opened mouth.

- Current Location: Museo de Antropologia de Xalapa.

San Lorenzo Monument 5 – Colossal Head 5

- Discovery: Yet another 1946 discovery by Stirling, found face-down on the southern section of the San Lorenzo mound. This was another masterpiece by the sculptors and was well preserved too, but the back of the head was slightly damaged. The point where it was found seems to be the original location based on the ceramic material found there.

- Size: the stone weighs 11.6 tons, 1.86 meters/6.1ft high, measuring 1.47 meters/4.8ft wide and 1.15 meters/3.8ft deep.

- Material/Dating: Based on the materials found at the particular site of Headstone 5, it was dated to San Lorenzo and Villa Alta phases of 1,400 – 1000 and 800 – 1000 AD

- Description: The head represents the face of an older adult with evident sleep bags below his eyes and an aging line that runs across the nose. The forehead shows an unmistakable frown. The parted lips did not reveal the teeth.

- Current Location: Colossal stone head 5 has been moved to the Museo de Antropologia de Xalapa in Mexico for display and other Olmec collections.

San Lorenzo Monument 17 – Colossal Head 6

•Discovery: This stone head is one of the smaller ones and was discovered by a local farmer before it was later excavated in 1965 by Roman Pina Chan and Luis Aveleyra. It was found looking downward.

•Size: it weighs about 8 to 10 tons, 1.67 meters/5.5ft high, 1.41 meters/4.6ft wide, and 1.26 meters/4.1ft deep.

•Description: The face shows some incongruity in shape, which could have only been due to an error by the sculptor or damage in transit. The character is an older male, with aging lines under the eyes and across the face; extra skin can be seen beneath the eyes, indicating old age.

•Current Location: it was first moved to the Metropolitan Museum of Art in New York but was returned to Mexico in 1970 to be the Museo Nacional Antropologia.

San Lorenzo Monument 53 – Colossal Head 7

●Discovery: It was discovered by a team of archaeologists from Yale University and Instituto Nacional de Antropologia de Historica. It is evident that it was a reworked job from the original form of a monumental stone throne. The stone was found face-up and slightly buried by erosion; also, not only was it poorly preserved, it had suffered obvious and deliberate damages.

●Size: Weighs 18 tons, 2.7meters/8.9ft high, 1.85meters/6.1ft wide, and 1.35meters/4.4ft deep.

●Description: It seems the mouth was carved to be open, but the lips are badly destroyed. The entire face is covered with wrinkles, indicating the character of a much older male with sagging cheeks and deep-set eyes.

●Current Location: Stone head 7 is currently sitting at the Museo de Antropologia de Xalapa, Mexico.

San Lorenzo Monument 61 – Colossal Head 8

•Discovery: This particular stone head has been described by many as one of the best works of art by the Olmecs. It was discovered on the southern part of the monumental throne lying on its side. The actual discovery occurred while a magnetometer survey of the site was being conducted in 1968, and it looked like it was reburied after the initial unrecorded discovery. Also, it is one of the well-preserved stone heads that didn't suffer any physical damage.

•Size: This stone head weighs 13 tons, standing at 2.2 meters/7.2ft high, measuring 1.65meters/5.4ft wide by 1.6 meters/5.2ft deep.

•Dating: it has been dated back to the Pre-Classic period.

•Description: Again, like the other stones, it's the face of a matured adult character with its forehead revealing an unmistakable frown, mouth slightly open to reveal the dental setting. While the face seems to have been carved out of natural material, the ears were represented by a single question mark shape.

•Current Location: The stone head was moved to the Museo de Antropologia de Xalapa in 1986. It still sits today, along with other discovered Colossal Head stones from the Olmec era.

San Lorenzo Monument 66 – Colossal Head 9

• Discovery: Stone head 9 was one of the most accessible finds because it seemed like it was exposed by erosion of the gully around the location of the head, but the date of discovery was put at 1982. It was found leaning on the right side and upwards with signs of erosion on the face.

• Size: it weighs about 10 tons, standing at 1.65 meters/5.4ft high, 1.36 meters/4.5ft wide, and 1.17 meters/3.8ft deep.

• Description: This head stone was carved, revealing this character as one who wears a piece of nose jewelry with a wrinkled face – but smiling, unlike most previous heads. It also has wide eyes and sagging cheeks. The only noticeable damage was to the upper lip. It was also mutilated with nine strange dents to the headdress.

• Current Location: Stone head 9 was left at the point of discovery for a while before it was eventually moved to Museo de Antropologia de Xalapa

San Lorenzo Monument 89 – Colossal Head 10

- Discovery: This stone head was discovered in a canyon in 1994 with the help of a magnetometer and eventually excavated by Ann Cyphers. The way it was found looked like it was buried lying face up.

- Size: it weighs about 8 tons, stands at 1.8 meter/5.9ft high, 1.43 meters/4.7ft by 0.92 meters/3ft deep.

- Description: This stone head has three unique tiny lines (like a bird's foot) on the forehead, with large ears extending further than the headdress. The face is a fully-grown adult, with sagging cheeks, a closed mouth, and revealing some lines under the eyes. Extra care seems to have gone into carving the lips, as they are very pronounced.

- Current Location: Stone Head 10 has since been moved to the Museo Comunitario se San Lorenzo Tenochtitlan around Texistepec.

The Famous Ball Game

So much has been said about the famous Mesoamerican ball game. The sport has cut across all classes in the region. This ball game has been traced back to 1400 BCE and is possibly the first team sport in history. The Olmecs have been identified as the first society to play this game from 1200 – 400 BCE. It was from them the game spread to the rest of the Mesoamerican region. However, it remains unclear if they were responsible for creating the game or copied it from other cultures outside of the region.

The Mayans were also known to have played the famous ball game in the Classical Maya, but they named theirs "pitz." The Aztec would later play the same ball game and called it "ollamalitli," a traditional Aztec name. The fact that the ball is made of rubber is the more reason why many believed it must have originated from the Olmecs, who have been tagged the "rubber people" or "people of the rubber name."

Interestingly the same ball game is still being played today in many parts of Mexico but with some modification and a new name called "ulama." Historically, this sport has been in existence for more than 3,400 years, making it the oldest sport because it has survived many generations – and still counting. It's also important to mention that it's the first ball game to use rubber in its ball.

The Rules of the Game and Gambling

As we have noticed, different civilizations have a separate name for the ball, but the general name back in the Mesoamerican era was "ulli." The game's rules seem pretty simple but achieving the goal – now, that's the challenging part!

The target of the players is to shoot the rubber ball through a vertical hoop (about 35" wide), such hoop being elevated. Although the ball was made from rubber, it still weighed about 4.1 kilos or 9 pounds. The field where the sporting action takes place is called "tlachtili," and covered an area of 100 to 300 feet long with erected walls on both sides where the stone rings hung.

The standard court had the shape of an "I" with a long line that runs through the middle of the tlachtili, and from that long line, there are sloping floors that meet the walls.

(from Wikipedia:
*https://en.wikipedia.org/wiki/Mesoamerican_ballgame#/media/File:Pok_ta_*
pok_ballgame_maya_indians_mexico_3.JPG)

Players would be penalized for using any part other than their head, legs, elbows, or hips when passing the ball, and the ball was not allowed to touch the ground. Any team that got the ball through the brick rings won! Due to the height of the hoop, which was about 20 feet off the ground, the game proved difficult, but there were other ways teams could score points. Any team that hit one of the six markers on the edges of the tlachtili would score points.

Though money had not yet emerged – and just like today – sports and betting were hard to separate. Gambling was a major aspect of the ball game, and it was recorded that the people gambled with anything and everything possible to entertain themselves. For example, some ancient folks used precious objects like Obsidian, feathers, and fine ceramics, while others gambled their wives, children, or even their lives! To put it simply, many winners took charge of the loser – his property and any other "asset."

Rewards for Winning and Losing

Sports served different purposes in each society. For some, it was mere entertainment or a means of unifying the people, while for others, the ball game had more religious relevance with severe consequences.

Some civilizations presented the winners with trophies that have been carved into the shape of a human head, called "hacha." There is speculation that earlier hachas might have been actual human heads. Palma was likely the costume that the players might have worn or used as ceremonial attire. The game gear worn was often protective because of the high risk involved. For example, the size and weight of the ball have been known to break the bones of players.

There are other types of trophies presented to winners in the form of stone yokes tied around the waist, on the arm, and in the form of rings. Most of these trophies often ended up in the grave with the individuals that won them. Some believe they were used to buy safe passage to the "other side."

Some of the religious and ritual aspects of the game involve sacrificing the team leader or, in some cases, the entire losing team to some form of deity. These sacrificial rituals were seen on courts at El Tajib and Chichen Itza, where losing teams were found having lost their limbs. Another fate of the losing team is evidenced by the presence of *tzompantli* (a large tray where skulls of the dead were showcased); in this way, players were made aware of their possible fate should they lose!

The Fall of San Lorenzo

After what seems like a glorious start and achieving the status of being the center of the Olmec civilization, San Lorenzo eventually fell and lost its glory. The situation is so bad that no one can accurately say what was responsible for the city's demise.

For example, Coe and Diehl initially submitted that the city's fall might have been as a result of internal fighting and possible invasion by neighboring cities, but Diehl has since backed away from that conclusion. In explaining his new position, Diehl believes that the state of the stone heads that were being recurved and reused before being dumped could not have been a result of warfare. Another renowned archaeologist and Professor of Anthropology at the University of Florida, Dr. David C. Grove, said,

> *"...almost nothing is known of their 'demise,' but because Olmec is an archaeological culture defined by certain artifacts, the 'end' of the Olmec is merely the disappearance of that artifact complex. There is no data to indicate whether the decline of the major Olmec centers and the disappearance of the defining artifacts complex was rapid or gradual. The late Pre-Classic monuments at Tres Zapotec strongly suggest that over time, the Olmec simply evolved out of the traits by which they were originally defined. Whatever the case, their legacy is most clearly found in the rulership monuments of the Classic period Maya."*

Other theories include the drastic climate change, which was a common occurrence around that time. Maybe the people abandoned the city when the condition became unbearable. Others opine that the likelihood of an epidemic was responsible for the decline of San Lorenzo – but there's no evidence to support that either.

Research is ongoing. Perhaps we'll learn why San Lorenzo fell to its knees after rising to such height and attaining the center's status to one of the world's most advanced civilizations of that time.

Chapter 8 – The Rise of La Venta

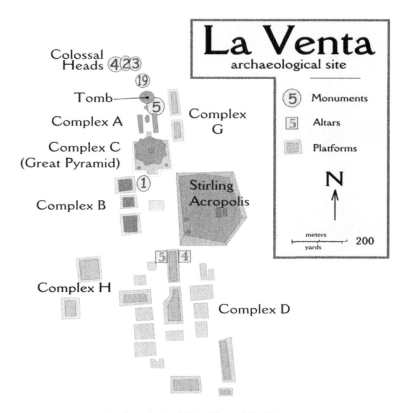

Archaeological Site Plan of La Venta

La Venta is a significant historical site in Mesoamerica between 800 and 400 BCE, part of the Middle Pre-classic period. This ancient Olmec settlement came as a replacement for San Lorenzo after its fall in the 10th century BCE. The site was occupied for 500 years before its abandonment at the beginning of the 4th century BCE.

La Venta was discovered in 1925 by archaeologists Frans Blom and Olivier La Farge. It was initially thought to be a Mayan site until radiocarbon techniques advanced. The archaeological site is now known for its planned layout, massive stone monuments, and the Great Pyramid. In addition, it has provided the most important archaeological finds from ancient Mesoamerica.

Geographical Location of La Venta

La Venta is located in present-day Tabasco, Mexico, close to its Gulf Coast. It was built on an island surrounded by the Tonalá River. The river currently divides the Mexican states of Veracruz and Tabasco.

La Venta spans about 16 kilometers inland and is less than 10 meters above sea level. It contains a little above 5.2 square kilometers of dry land, surrounded by vegetation and water bodies.

The Structure of La Venta

Most of the structures from La Venta were built from earth and clay. Only a few used basalt, andesite, and limestone in the foundations. One beautiful thing about the site is its well-planned layout. The main structures are oriented 8^0 west of north and are believed to be aligned with some star or constellation. The structures located on the east and west sides are similarly set.

Only a few of the residential structures in La Venta have survived.

The Great Pyramid of La Venta

Complex C, The Great Pyramid of La Venta

The Great Pyramid is the major La Venta structure and is found at the site's center. It is shaped like a fluted cone. Also referred to as Complex C, it is one of the oldest pyramids known in Mesoamerica. The structure is a high clay mound with a length of 110 feet and an estimated 100,000 cubic meters. It was once thought to be created after the shape of a volcano or mountain. However, recent research shows that it was previously a rectangular pyramid, and the present shape is attributed to the 2500 years of erosion.

On the southern side of the pyramid is a deviation from the standard shape. It is believed to be an area of burned clay, a stock of buried offerings, or a tomb. The date of the Great Pyramid was determined through radiocarbon dating to be between 364-424 BCE.

Complex A

Complex A, La Venta

Complex A is located north of the Great Pyramid and comprises about three acres. It consists of mounds (heap of earth or rock) and plazas (open areas), surrounded by basalt columns which probably denotes limited access. The mounds were burial and ceremonial structures.

Underneath the mounds and plazas in Complex A are a variety of offerings and buried objects, including jade ornaments and polished mirrors. Five huge offerings made of serpentine blocks were also buried, one of which consisted of 50 tons of serpentine blocks covered in 4000 tons of clay.

Also excavated from complex A are three rectangular mosaic pavements representing jaguar masks. Each of the pavements measured 15 by 20 feet and consisted of 485 blocks of serpentine. After their completion, these structures were buried intentionally by covering them with clay and earth.

Located north of the Great Pyramid is also a ceremonial enclosure containing several tombs where deceased Olmec rulers were buried. The site consisted of five formal tombs, each with unique details while still maintaining the sites' structure.

Complex B

Complex B is located south of the Great Pyramid. Its plaza appears to be specially built for public gatherings. The plaza is about 400 meters long and over 100 meters wide and located in the southern part of what is known as the "great pyramid," and from the Stirling Acropolis, it is toward the west; but from the Complex B Platform, it is situated toward the east. The Stirling Acropolis was given the name as a mark of honor to the great work done by Stirling and his team as the first archaeologist to work on La Venta as far back as the 1940s.

Based on the details that went into the layout, Mesoamerican historians believed the platforms around the plaza were used as some sort of stages where religious and rituals are carried out. Complex B contained numerous monuments and a large plaza, and it is believed to have served as the primary site where La Venta rulers carry out ritual performances. The rituals carried out were possibly related to the Altars, Stelae (sculpted stone slabs with figures or inscriptions), and Monuments found in the area. The sculptures were placed in such a way that they could easily convey their messages to the audience.

Complex E

While there are currently no buildings in this area, analysis of the soil revealed the possibility that it had been a residential zone.

In total, seventy-seven carved stone monuments have been found in La Venta. They include four colossal heads, four multi-ton greenstone offerings, three mosaic pavements of serpentine blocks, a tomb of basalt columns, and numerous small jade figures and ornaments. The location of La Venta made it impossible to have natural stones and basalts like in San Lorenzo, the previous Olmec center. Therefore, there was a limitation of stone monuments; the ones found at the site mostly came from the Tuxtla Mountains in Cerro Cintepec.

Colossal Heads

Colossal heads, made from basalt, are the most popular of the La Venta monuments. Four colossal heads were found on the site and were officially called, Monuments 1-4. Monument 1 was located south of the Great Pyramid. And monuments 2 to 4 were located north of Complex A. The heads weighed about 18 tons, with a maximum height of 9 feet 4 inches. It is unsure how the Olmecs moved such huge stones. They were believed to be carved as early as 850 BCE.

The colossal heads were sculpted from basalt boulders. The facial features such as eyes, mouth, nostrils, cheeks, lips – and sometimes dimples – were drilled into the stone. These heads are striking because the Olmecs did not have any metal tools and used hard hand-held stones for sculpting.

Most Colossal Heads are taller than an average human being and consist only of a head and face. The back of the heads is flat, denoting that the sculptures were created to be viewed only from the front and sides. The sculptures also include a helmet similar to the American football helmet of the 1920s. Each sculpture is unique, with distinct features indicating that they were humans that existed. Most archaeologists today think that the heads represent highly esteemed Olmec rulers with great power.

Some theories suggest that the heads signified rulership and were placed in specific sites to show political dominance. The four heads of La Venta were initially positioned facing outwards as if they were guarding the vicinity.

The colossal heads are of great importance to both researchers and modern Mexicans, revealing more about the Olmec culture. They are also an intriguing attraction to many visitors and are currently found in museums close to the La Venta site.

Altars

Altar 4, La Venta

They are also referred to as *thrones* and were carved from basalt stones. Seven basalt altars were found in La Venta, and they depict the rulers during important rituals or ceremonies. The common ones are altars 4 and 5.

Altar 4 shows a figure sitting at the mouth of a cave and holding a rope with his hands – a rope that winds around the bottom of the altar to another figure. It is believed that the sculpture suggests a ruler taking hostages to sacrifice them to the gods. On the other hand, some believe that the figures attached to the rope are ancestors aiding the ruler.

Altar 5 has a very close resemblance to Altar 4 in design and construction, but the carved figure is holding what looks like a baby were-jaguar.

Matthew Stirling takes a photo with Altar 5

Other Artifacts

Jade Ornaments

Offering #4 from La Venta is a group of small stone figures also known as jade ornaments. The celts are thin, smooth structures ground from stone and tapered at one or both ends. The group consisted of 17 images arranged straight facing upwards right in front of the jade celts. While one of the figures was made of eroded granite, others were made of greenstone. Greenstone was highly valued among Olmecs and consisted of green and bluish-green rocks.

The head of the figures appears elongated. The face contains eyes that look swollen and have an almond shape. Additionally, the nostrils and ears were drilled for appropriate representation. The knees and elbows are slightly bent with a hand on each side of the figure. The figures look similar but are unique in features like height, color, and facial features.

The figures and the celts were used to create scenes. Most scholars believe that Offering #4 represents a mythological or historical scene – a ritual to honor a dignitary, a meeting to carry out a human sacrifice, or a marriage ceremony. It was also confirmed that the celts are backdrops and represent Stelae, showing that the site is of great importance to the people.

Polished Iron Ore Mirrors

These mirrors were fashioned from iron ore, mainly hematite, ilmenite, and magnetite. They were polished to give a reflective surface. The mirrors also had holes close to their edges, indicating that they had been worn as chest ornaments. These mirrors were majorly excavated from offerings; seven were unearthed from Complex A at La Venta. Mirrors were a significant part of the Olmecs and were used in rituals and daily lives.

Religion

Specific patterns in the Olmec culture were symbolic with probable ritual meaning. A symbol showing an 'X' in a rectangular box has been seen in La Venta stones and was passed on to cultures inspired by Olmecs.

Also, some Olmec arts show a relationship between animals and spirituality, as evidenced in elites wearing headdresses having feathers and other animal forms. Additionally, shark teeth and stingray remains were found at feasting sites at San Andrés.

Artifacts found at La Venta formed a part of their religion. Celts and jade ornaments were offered to deities during ceremonies. Iron ore mirrors were also used during rituals. In addition, the Olmecs believed in supernatural beings, as seen in some of their artifacts.

La Venta as a Ceremonial and Civic Center

La Venta was mainly dominated by Complex A, the Great Pyramid, and the large plaza to their south. The site's unique design shows the relevance of the ruler's role in mediating between the water and earth realm.

The site had various agricultural and marine resources, and a large number of the La Venta occupants were fishermen and agriculturalists. As a result, they made their homes close to the creeks and rivers that surrounded La Venta. So, based on the location of their settlement, they naturally depended on marine life like fish, shellfish, and others, but they later shifted to maize, palm, kinds of cotton, bears, and other farm produce grown primarily on gardens and small ridges.

The Great Pyramid divides La Venta into northern and southern sectors. It is believed that access to the northern ceremonial sector of Complex A was limited to the elite. As for commoners, they habited distant sites such as San Andrés. Unlike what we found in another part of the region where there were dedicated places for burial, La Venta had tombs and monuments strategically arranged and located in the mounds and platform, and many buried offerings were found in these platforms.

Worthy of note is that La Venta had skilled craftsmen who created the unique monuments that La Venta is known for today. A cylinder seal and other forms of writing were also found on the site showing that a writing system existed in La Venta.

Excavations and Current La Venta Site

Excavators of the La Venta site were members of the Smithsonian Institution and included Matthew Stirling, Philip Drucker, Waldo Wedel, and Robert Heizer. The excavations were mainly carried out between 1942 and 1955, after which the site was extensively damaged by looting and civic development. Furthermore, a three-dimensional map of Complex A was designed by Gillespie and Volk and published in 2014.

Most of the archaeological sites were destroyed due to the construction of a nearby petroleum refinery and the removal of significant monuments without any markers to signify their original locations. As a result, excavations are now challenging to carry out. Several artifacts have been moved from their original location and other places like the Parque Museo La Venta, also known as the La Venta Museum. The museum's location is in Villa Hermosa (in modern-day Tabasco), and the site is now protected as an archaeological park.

Chapter 9 – Custom and Society

Olmec, Long-count Calendar

The status of the Olmecs as the first society to develop in the Americas make it essential for us to dive into the customs and type of society that the people had. The progressive advancement of the Olmec has been divided into:

1. Early Formative 1800 to 900 BCE
2. Middle Formative 900 to 400 BCE
3. Late/Terminal Formative 400 BCE to 200 CE.

Scholars often used the phrase "mother culture" to describe the Olmec because their culture and civilization were not only the first to stand out, but it spread all through the Mesoamerican region, and the influence was evident in several societies. This influence was so profound that, at some point, some scholars attributed the civilization seen in the region to the Mayans and Aztecs. That error has since been corrected.

Coming from a society that was mostly known to rely on agriculture on the Gulf Lowlands from as far back as 1600 BCE, during the Early Formative periods, the culture had massive influence and control in the Olmec heartlands, which was located on the southern Gulf of Mexico and the shores in Tabasco and Veracruz. The first known Olmec center was San Lorenzo which falls into modern-day Veracruz.

While San Lorenzo reigned as the major Olmec center around 1200 BCE, La Venta began to grow. While the Olmec culture was notably practiced there, it never reached nor came close to the level of development seen in San Lorenzo until around 900 BCE. Then like San Lorenzo, after 500 years of occupation, La Venta too was abandoned around the early part of the 4th century.

From its coastal location on an island in a swamp looking over Rio Palma, evidence found at the site revealed that La Venta did more than influence the cultures of surrounding cities but had political control over some part of the region between Mezcalapa and Coatzacoalcos Rivers.

It is not surprising that the La Venta Olmecs transitioned from relying on seafood to agriculture. Much has been said about the strategic location of the city. For Example, the La Venta is located among different types of ecosystems like a tropical forest (where they could clear lands for farming), marshes, swamps, and the Gulf of Mexico. The humid climate with an annual temperature of 26 Degrees Celsius and nearly 2,000 millimeters of annual rainfall made the ground perfect for farming.

The archaeological site at La Venta had many residential buildings, which could only have indicated the population expansion the cities experienced. At the same time, it was regarded as the new Olmec center. Some of these residential buildings have survived through many centuries and still exist at the site today. It was observed that there were no structures dedicated to food production, religious, economic, and military operations. The main La Venta site is a complex made from clay and constructed stretching 20Km towards the north-south, while the site is designed from west to north.

As mentioned earlier, there was a limited supply of stones and rocks in La Venta, so the people relied more on clay for their residential buildings and other structures. That is much different from what was obtainable at the Maya and among the Aztecs. The large basalt stones found at the site were not used to build residential apartments but used strictly for carving monuments like Colossal Heads, altars, several stelae, and stone thrones. That is the extent of the scarcity of stone and rock at the site. The little that was available was brought in and used wisely. A good example was the basalts columns deposited at Complex A; they did not originate from within the city but could have come from nearby places like Punta Roca Partida, in San Andres.

How the mounds, residential buildings, complexes, and monuments at La Venta were arranged provides insight into the unique ceremonial nature of the city. In the words of Rebecca Gonzalez-Lauck, "one of the earliest examples of large-scale ideological communications through the interaction of architecture and sculpture." Rebecca is an Award-Winning Mexican Archaeologist.

Social Structure at La Venta

The social structure of La Venta had power concentration; likewise, the level architecture, type of artifacts, and luxury items found at the site speak volumes. Among the cities that represented the culture and civilization of the Olmecs, La Venta was the largest of them all and adopted a complex royal system based on hierarchy made up of the ruler, the elites, and the ruled. In the midst of all these was the priest, who was believed to be the mouthpiece of the gods and had power over life and death and, in some instances, *political influence.* The actual political structure the Olmecs adopted is still unclear, but new findings and dating would probably shed more light on this elusive, most advanced civilization.

"The nature of the political organization and social integration of Olmec centers remains a point of scholarly contention. General consensus advocates the notion of a theocratic chiefdom. Such a sociopolitical system involves governance of each center by a single, elite individual, or chief, who exercises authority over all things religious and monetary. With respect to the former, artistic representations' iconographic symbols and motifs suggest that the Olmecs practiced a religion distinguished by shamanism. Shamans, or shamanic chiefs, mediated between the natural, earthly realm and the supernatural realm of the ancestors and deities. As first pointed out by Peter Furst in 1968, Olmec sculpture also depicts shamans' supernatural power and ability to transform from human to animal spirits. Use of psychotropic drugs may have facilitated shamanic transformations. Aside from religious activities, the chief's monetary responsibilities were related to food production and collection of tribute. An elite minority, presumably related to the chief, would have also exercised economic control over food tribute and trade networks. Trade with Mesoamerican groups distant from the Olmec is evidenced by materials such as blue-green jade from the Motagua Valley in Guatemala, fine white kaolin clay from Chalcatzingo, magnetite from the Valley of Oaxaca, and obsidian from central Mexico and the Maya highlands. Interactions via trade would have afforded the opportunity for communication of religious, social, and political ideas as well.

Much of this dialogue between the Olmecs and their distant Mesoamerican neighbors is supported by the appearance of Olmec art, or local expressions with characteristic features, in widely dispersed locales. Olmec art possesses distinctive stylistic traits that first appeared in the Olmec heartland between 1250-1150 B.C. Rulership and shamanism are the dominant themes. Most notable for their size and early dates are the three-dimensional human figures carved from stone. These include colossal basalt stone heads, seated and kneeling individuals, throne-like altars, and stelae. The effort that would have been required to procure enormous basalt boulders from their source, the Tuxtlas Mountains, cannot be overstated. First reported in 1862 at the site of Hueyapan in Veracruz, colossal stone heads were, in fact, investigators' earliest exposure to Olmec culture. Scholars have convincingly argued that carved heads portray individual Olmec leaders. Often these monuments were found defaced or intentionally broken, which possibly signified the cessation of a leader's rule or life. Olmec-style art is also found on a considerably smaller scale, as exemplified by portable artifacts." Extracted from Anthropology – Olmecs.

Some artifacts and signs found on them were an indication of classes that existed. For example, the feathered headdresses, type of jewelry, and the specific body part where the jewelry was worn are good indicators. Wearing a mirror was very common among some elite, and you could tell it had a special place in the people's culture. Luxury and other objects with high value attached to them were a sign of economic, political, royal, and religious power in the La Venta polity. The rulers and elite used all these to command power and demanded respect from the lower class in the city.

Several scholars and archaeologists agree that at the peak of the reigns of La Venta, the population would have been up to 18,000 people. In addition to the mysteries of La Venta, the sand at the site did not preserve the remains of people buried, which made it nearly impossible to identify the differences in burial arrangement and locations at the site. However, the Colossal Heads found at various site locations support evidence that the elite had a firm grip over the lower class. Furthermore, constructing a residential abode for the elite would have involved massive labor with many people from the lower class.

Recent excavations have also revealed how the city must have been divided into some parts, especially the best part of the city, reserved for the elites and the less productive part for the lower class. All these were indications that social classes existed; therefore, social inequality must have been the order of the day – and part of the complexity of the La Venta Olmecs.

Burials Sites and Rituals

Buried Mosaics or Pavements from La Venta, consisting of nearly 500 blocks of serpentine

Among the many discoveries at the La Venta site are burial places, especially in locations like Mound A, but the environment made it impossible to support to preserve any form of remains because organic material doesn't do well with the type of acidic soil found in La Venta. The only signs of remains the site had to offer were found in a basalt tomb and contained:

- A burnt skullcap
- Shark tooth
- Stingray spines
- Some milk teeth

There was a high concentration of some items like jade celts at these burials places, and it would look like they were a form of requirement for ritual purposes for a particular class of people, but no human remains were found so, it was difficult to confirm this. Other artifacts include beads, plaques, jewelry, obsidian, earspools, spangles, and rare items. Whether they fell off the bodies of decomposed people buried there or were placed there as ritual rites remain to be seen, but one thing was sure, it was a common find at several burial sites.

Structure A-2 – Mound A

The platform is made of clay and looks very much like a burial site. Within the platform were decomposed bones of human remains that were poorly preserved, and items found there include cinnabar, a red paint-like substance commonly used in the region to indicate status. Also found on the platform were jade, masks, and figurines, along with mirrors and obsidian, which have long been established as class items among the elites.

For example, the mirror carried a special significance meaning it mainly was worn or used by the royals, priests, and the elite. It was not particularly common among the lower class of the Olmecs. The stelae and other relevant carvings and monuments showed several Olmec leaders wearing them on their chest, forehead, and arms. The nature of the burials found inside the platform shows that the corpses might have been wrapped before being buried.

Urn Burials

The urn burial was discovered in Complex E, which was more of a residential area in the city. Also found were pieces of bones and teeth, all buried in ceramic pots. According to Rust, *"The fill immediately around this large urn was clean, yellow sand, and the urn was covered with an inverted fine-paste orange bowl with flaring walls; the bowl's interior was painted red and incised with the double-line-break pattern on the inside rim."*

Like many things from the Olmecs, this system of managing a complex society by breaking it into classes was replicated in several civilizations in Mesoamerica. Classes were noticed all over the region, and the priest and royals were treated and semi-gods. They, in turn, ruled and controlled the people using fear and manipulation. From places of abode to final resting places, the gap among the class kept widening. It all started with the Olmecs and was then passed down to other cultures that followed.

Chapter 10 – Economy and Religion

The Olmecs laid the foundation for artistic innovation in Mesoamerica. The artifacts discovered there still help in understanding what they believed and how they lived. The Olmecs built their economy by exporting some of these products while importing those they did not have.

The Economy of La Venta

Basalt rocks used in the creation of stone monuments were brought in from the Tuxtla mountains. It's been suggested that the rocks were traded with another culture, but it is still uncertain.

From the well-sculpted stone monuments seen in La Venta, the site used many highly skilled artisans. The Olmecs also created elegant vessels and ceramic figures out of clay. There is a possibility that more goods were exported than imported. And this could have led to the Olmecs building their relationships with other cultures. These resulted in the elites possessing significant power with luxury goods and feasting foods like cocoa and maize beer.

Agriculture in La Venta

La Venta had a wide variety of plants and animals. The animals were mostly sea animals, deer, and other small animals. La Venta and its surrounding sites mainly depended on hunting wild animals. Dogs were the only animals domesticated by the Olmec.

Due to the rich, alluvial soil located along the river banks, La Venta had a bountiful harvest every year. Maize was the primary plant they cultivated.

Religion and Rituals

Monument 19, a feathered serpent

Some patterns seen in La Venta have been thought to have a ritual meaning. An example is the crossed band symbol which appears as an 'X' in a rectangular box. Many stones in La Venta and other Olmec sites have been found to possess this symbol.

The religious activities of the Olmec were performed by rulers, priests, and shamans. The rulers appear to be the most important religious figures because of their connection to Olmec deities. It is believed that the Olmecs had different supernatural beings, as evidenced in Olmec artifacts.

Olmec Dragon (Earth Monster)

It is portrayed as a crocodile-like being with flaming eyebrows around the nose and its tongue split in two. The Earth Monster also has prominent fangs (long, pointed teeth). His mouth, sometimes open, is seen as a cave. In the Olmec culture, it is one of the supernatural beings most commonly depicted, thought to represent agriculture, fertility, and fire.

Maize Deity

Maize was an essential and common crop to the Olmecs, so it is not surprising that they assigned a god to it. The Maize Deity is identified by maize growing from his cleft head. It is usually seen in the figures of rulers. A carved celt (originally found in Veracruz) shows a depiction of the Maize Deity.

Rain Spirit and Were-Jaguar

In 1955, Matthew Stirling proposed that Were-Jaguar resulted from a mating between a jaguar and a woman. From that time, any figure showing almond-shaped eyes, downturned mouth, and a cleft head were described as a "Were-Jaguar."

Some researchers believe that the rain spirit and Were-Jaguar are the same. Others believe that they are two separate supernatural beings. It is suggested that the Olmec rain spirit had Were-Jaguar features and had other attributes, including a headband, headdress, pleated ear bars, and a "crossed bar"' icon on the chest/or navel.

Banded-Eye God

The banded-eye god has a cleft head and a downturned mouth. The eyes are almond-shaped with a narrow band or stripe that runs along the side of its face. The banded-eye god appears more human than other Olmec gods. It is represented on the famous Olmec Statue, Las Limas Monument 1.

Feathered Serpent

Feathered or plumed serpent, now known throughout Mesoamerica, first appeared in Olmec culture. It is seen as a rattlesnake with feathers on its head. It is represented in Monument 19 from La Venta. Though not very common in Olmec arts, later equivalents such as the Aztec deity, Quetzalcoatl, and the Maya deity, Kukulkan, had a more important place in Mesoamerican religion.

Fish or Shark Monster

Monument 58 is one of the artifacts used to depict the Fish Monster. It has also appeared in stone carvings, pottery, and celts and represents the underworld. Its shark tooth and monster-like head identify the Fish Monster. It also possesses "crossed bands," a dorsal fin, and a split tail. Shark teeth uncovered from some Olmec sites show that the Fish Monster was honored in some rituals.

Bird Monster

The Bird Monster is portrayed as a frightening bird, sometimes with features of a reptile. It is usually found in the carved figures of rulers, especially in their dresses. The bird monster image also appears on many other artifacts, including on a crucial altar.

Animals and Spirituality

The Olmecs paid special significance to jaguars, eagles, caimans, snakes, and sharks. Numerous artifacts from Olmecs show animal characteristics combined with human features, and there seems to be a connection between animals and spirituality among the Olmecs. For example, Olmec elites wore headdresses with feathers and other animal forms.

Some sea creatures were also sacred to the Olmec. Shark teeth and stingrays have been found at feasting sites in San Andres, a nearby elite center. It is also clear that those in La Venta shared the same ideology.

Olmec Artifacts

The different artifacts found in La Venta have been of great importance in understanding the Olmec religion. There is no ideal strategy for fully understanding the Olmec artifacts due to the lack of written documents – most of what is known as a result of repeated patterns that are symbolic.

Many of the pieces initially located at La Venta have been moved to the La Venta Park in Villahermosa, Mexico. Tabasco poet, Carlos Pellicer, championed the movement, designing, organizing, and assembling the park in 1957. Pellicer began to rescue many archaeological pieces from La Venta when he discovered that the site was being destroyed by the petroleum refinery built near it. He also placed them in a natural environment as they were supposed to be when they were found.

More than 50 Olmec artifacts are present in La Venta Park. The park presents a jungle-like environment similar to the original La Venta site.

Jade ornaments

Offering #4 from La Venta is a group of small stone figures also known as jade ornaments. This group consisted of seventeen figures placed upright arranged in front of six jade celts. While one of the figures was made of eroded granite, others were made of greenstone. Greenstone was highly valued among Olmecs and consisted of green and bluish-green stones. The celts are thin, smooth structures ground from stone and tapered at one or both ends.

The head of the figures appears elongated. The face contains eyes that look swollen and have an almond shape. Additionally, the nostrils and ears are drilled for appropriate representation. The knees and elbows are slightly bent with a hand on each side of the figure. The figures look similar but are unique in features like height, color, and facial features.

The figures and the celts were used to create scenes. Most scholars believe that Offering #4 represents a mythological or historical scene – a ritual to honor a dignitary, a meeting to carry out a human sacrifice, or a marriage ceremony. It was also confirmed that the celts are backdrops and represent Stelae, showing that the site is of great importance.

Polished Iron Ore Mirrors

These mirrors were fashioned from iron ore, mainly hematite, ilmenite, and magnetite. They were polished to give a reflective surface. The mirrors also had holes close to their edges, indicating that they had been worn as chest ornaments. Fragments of this mirror have been discovered in abundance in La Venta. They were majorly excavated from offerings; seven were unearthed from Complex A at La Venta. Mirrors seemed to have been very significant in the Olmec culture and were used in rituals and daily life.

Celts or "Pseudo axes"

They are made of jade. Most are smooth, but a few are decorated with what are thought to be religious symbols.

They were very common in both burials and offerings. Together with jade offerings, celts were offered to deities during ceremonies at La Venta.

Stelae

Stelae are stone monuments that have sculpted elements on them. In stela's, the sculpted elements are raised, and the background appears lower.

Stela 2 shows the figure of a King with multiple figures (supposedly bodyguards) protecting the King. The King is seen holding a staff of power and wearing a headdress. There are also representations of spikes or thunders on the sculpture.

Stela 3 shows two figures. One is a bearded, long nose man, known famously as the 'Uncle Sam' figure. It is believed that the sculpture represents the meeting of two dignitaries – the Olmec and another culture. The two figures are both standing on a sacred rock, sharing information. Some figures are seen floating or flying while the two are having their meeting.

Stela 19, found in the La Venta site, has been found to have a very unusual carving. The figure in the middle appears to hold something that looks like a bag, handle, or lever. The figure is also seen seated within the body of a plumed serpent. The serpent's head has a helmet with 'crossed bars,' typical of numerous Olmec monuments. The plumed serpent continues round the stela and ends in a rattlesnake tail.

Stela 19 is thought to be one of the first representations of Quetzalcoatl (Aztec deity), who first arrived on Mexico's Gulf coast and left the Serpent sanctuary many years later. The carving is assumed to be revering where Quetzalcoatl first arrived and where he left. It is vital in the Quetzalcoatl story; his link with the Olmec eventually spread onto the Aztec and Mayan world.

Basalt columns

Complex A, an area restricted to the elites, was surrounded by basalt columns. Basalt columns served as fences and were primarily used to delineate sacred precincts from public spaces. They were about 25 feet long and had strange cut marks on them.

Other Monuments

Monument 13

This monument was found close to the sacred precinct of La Venta. It is also known as 'The traveler.' The sculpture shows a figure wearing a turban and sandal, carrying something like a flag. It has been thought to represent a meeting with a different culture – someone who arrived in the Olmec world.

Monument 20

Monument 20 looks like a large piece of shark. It was made out of serpentine and is thought to represent marine life.

Monument 59

Monument 59 is a Were-Jaguar or Human-like Jaguar. Its limbs appear stretched out, holding a spherical object or a type of slab. The sculpture also has multiple marks and carvings.

Monument 63

Monument 63 shows a figure with a banner. The figure wears a headdress and has a beard. Above the individual is a great fish with massive jaws, dorsal fins, and teeth that suggest it could be a shark. The sculpture represents the great god Quetzalcoatl, or one of the many travelers in the Olmec world. At the back of the sculpture are several cut marks and indentations, probably representing several language systems.

Monument 64

Monument 64 appears to be ahead with a vast cleft in the middle of the skull. The aperture could also be a part of the helmet. The sculpture also had long thin eyes and an abnormal mouth. It is believed to represent a Were-Jaguar.

Monument 77

Monument 77 is also called "The Governor." It was seen at the entrance to the sacred precinct of La Venta and appeared to be guarding the Pyramid and sacred area. It looks like a classic kind of Egyptian-looking statue with a cloak at its back representing a jaguar. It also wears a headdress similar to those of the Egyptians.

Human figures or Deities?

Numerous important figures have been found in many stone monuments in La Venta. Scholars are still unsure which of them are human rulers or gods since there seems to be a slight difference between the deities and the Olmec rulers in their ideology.

Writing System in La Venta

The Olmec had a form of a writing system that used symbols. And this is seen in the cylinder seal and other forms of writing found at San Andreas.

Chapter 11 – Decline and the Epi-Olmecs

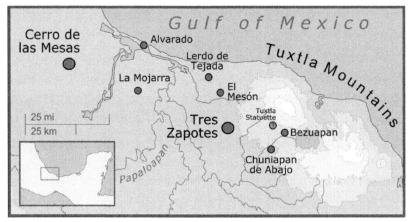

Important Epi-Olmec sites

We have earlier established that the Olmec culture was the first complex civilization that later spread throughout the Mesoamerican region. Along with their ways of life, the people thrived along the Gulf of Mexico from around 1200 to 400 BCE. Several scholars have described them as the forebearers of modern civilization and later societies, like the Mayan and Aztecs. The writing systems and calendar styles that we later saw in other emerging societies and improved by other cultures originated from the Olmecs.

However, at about 400 BCE, just like San Lorenzo, the Olmec city of La Venta declined after replacing San Lorenzo – which had served the people for 2000 years. The decline of the city took the Olmec

Classic Era along with it. The reason for the decline of La Venta, like the previous Olmec center, is still unclear, mainly because the city fell long before the arrival of the Europeans to the region.

As we now know, the two great Olmec cities of San Lorenzo and La Venta were named based on the location of archaeologist findings. Their original names have been lost in time and are still to be discovered. San Lorenzo enjoyed a great run as the epic center of the Olmec culture and was located on an island around 1200 to 900 BCE; then went into decline and was replaced by La Venta.

La Venta went into decline around 400 BCE and was abandoned entirely. The fall of the great city of La Venta also signified the end of the Classic Olmec culture. There are still remnants of La Venta scattered all over the region, but their culture is long lost and extinct. The Olmecs built and managed an extensive trade network while the cities were thriving, but all that fell apart as the city declined. All the unique items known with the culture, like pottery styles, sculptures, jades, which all had peculiar Olmec motifs, were no longer made.

Historians, researchers, and archaeologists specializing in Mesoamerican artifacts have not reached a consensus on precisely what happened to the Olmec civilizations or what caused them to decline. However, some think that it could be a combination of several things. For example, the society relied heavily on farming and some crops like maize, potatoes, and squash for their livelihood; this could have made them vulnerable to climate change. Some scholars are even of the opinion that a volcanic eruption could have covered the whole area in ash or even distorted the flow of water that comes from the river, thereby disrupting their irrigation system and eventually leading to famine.

There were also stories of an outbreak of an epidemic that could have wiped out the population. Artificial human actions were not left out of the theories because some believed that was war between La Venta and neighboring societies, and this could have led to the fall of the cities, but there is no evidence to support these stories, not even the signs of an internal war between the cities. The likely conclusion that most scholars are leaning towards in agreement is over farming, destruction of the forest for farming, and eventually climate change.

The Emergence of Epi-Olmec Culture

When La Venta, the last Olmec center, fell, the Olmec culture did not go into extinction; instead, it transitioned into what we now know as the Epi-Olmec culture. This was a connection between the original culture from the Classic era mixed with the culture of the people of Veracruz, and this is because the remnants of La Venta fled or moved to neighboring cities, especially Veracruz.

The remnants could not establish control of the Olmec culture in their newfound homes but coexisted with the people as they practiced a lighter version of what they used to have. The migrated Olmec and the Veracruz culture thrived along with the northern Olmec lands for another 500 years.

So, the Epi-Olmec culture emerged around the Formative Period and became successful in present-day Veracruz. They lived mainly along the Papaloapan River from around 300BCE to 250 CE. The Epi-Olmec culture never reached the height and achievement of the original culture, especially in the artifacts (like the Colossal Heads and other monuments), neither was it close in complexity. However, it did better than the original Olmec culture in the improvement of writing and calendar systems.

The cities that benefited from the influx of the original Olmec as La Venta fell include:

- Tres Zapotes
- Cerro de les Mesas
- El Tajin
- El Meson,
- Chunipan de Abajo
- Lerdo de Tejada

Among these cities, Tres Zapotes and Cerro de Mesas were the two cities with the lost glory of San Lorenzo and La Venta, the original Olmec centers. However, it was only a *look-alike;* they never came close to matching any of the fallen cities, but important artifacts found at the site, like improved writing system, calendrics, and astronomy, made them worthy of being studied.

Tres Zapotes

In January 1939, American and archaeologist Mathew Stirling and his wife, Marion Stirling (an authority like her husband), and a team of other archaeologists led another expedition to Veracruz, Mexico. The was just one of Stirling's 14 expeditions; he was already a known and respected name in different parts of the Americas. This particular venture was sponsored by a joint effort of the National Geographic Society and the Smithsonian Institution.

While exploring several mounds around the Arroyo Hueyapan in Tres Zapotes, right in front of the tallest mounds at that time, the team discovered carved rocked like a pillar, but it was a monument next to an ancient altar. The carved monolith, named Stela C, turned out to be one of the best discoveries of Stirling's work in the Americas. Stela C had a peculiar carving of a were-jaguar sculptured on it to the side, which looked closely like some of the discoveries at the major Olmec centers.

Also, the Mayan center was only a hundred miles away from the site of the discoveries. After a careful study of Stela C, archaeologists concluded that it had to be the symbol of authority for a powerful ruler that reigned in the city. In one part of the carving, Stirling saw what looked like a date from his experience with Maya inscriptions; it had bars and dots. He wrote out the numbers and took them to their camp to show his wife Marion, the expert at ancient American writing styles.

While attempting to translate the writing, Marion noticed that the top half of Stela C was missing, and it was the part that indicated that the period was called a Baktun. However, based on her experience, he guessed what it could mean and arrived at a date that reads: "3rd September, 32 BC." Three decades after her educated guess, Marion was validated when the top half was discovered; her date was accurate.

At the time of Stirling's finding, the Stela C was the earliest known Mesoamerican long-count calendar that existed, but several decades later, Stela 2, which was found at a small site named Chiapas de Corzo in Mexico, would later surpass Stirling's finding. Stela 2 was translated to have a confirmed date of 6th December 36 BCE. Additionally, when Stirling and his team discovered Stela C, they concluded that it was a Mayan-style long-count calendar dating system, hence an invention of the Mayans. However, the findings in Veracruz have debunked Stirling's conclusion and pushed the date further back in time. In essence, history has been re-written.

The expedition to Tres Zapotes was a rich find for Sterling and his team. It had a wealth of archaeological artifacts like several pieces of jades, thousands of fragments from the pottery system, and a few Colossal Heads similar to what had been found in San Lorenzo and other Olmec centers. Scholars believe that the wealth of discovery at the Tres Zapotec site further confirms that the city was occupied for more than 2000 years and probably the longest-occupied of all the Olmec Centers. That leads us to wonder: Who were these people are and how could they coexist for that long?

The Tres Zapotes archaeological site is currently located between the Papaloapan River basin and the Tuxtla Mountains and has access to the Veracruz lowlands swamps and the forested uplands. The mountains were primary sources of stone structures and sculptures, and the was a fairly regular supply of water running through Arroyo Hueyapan. The Tres Zapotes site has a daily temperature of 78 degrees which gives it a classification, "tropical monsoon," and farming was carried on all year round. The site was also a perfect location for trade networks, and evidence found at the site revealed that Tres Zapotes had trade dealings with other neighboring societies for the extended period it was occupied.

The gradual emergence of the Tres Zapotes site started when San Lorenzo (and later, La Venta) was experiencing a decline. Based on the archaeological findings at the Tres Zapotes, scholars put the date of founding the site at 1500 BCE, but it did not gain the status and authority of being the Olmec center until about 900 BCE – or what is known as the Middle Formative Period. The first architectural monumental building appeared around the same time – 500 BCE.

It remains unclear how Tres Zapotes became an Epi-Olmec center while previously great cities like San Lorenzo and La Venta fell. Some scholars believe that the city likely took in refugees from the fallen cities. Or perhaps the people just continued practicing the Olmec way of life even after the fall of the former Olmec centers. Whichever position you choose, one thing is clear, Tres Zapotes had remnants of the Olmecs, and they carried on the Olmec tradition while other centers suffered a decline.

Artifacts found at the site further proved that Tres Zapotes attained the status of being an Olmec center even though the complexity of the society tilted more towards that of the Mayans than the Aztecs *in the way the cities functioned*. Rather than have a central ruler, the cities were allowed to function as separate political entities. Additionally, evidence revealed that the political arrangement at Tres Zapotes was further broken down to ruling royal families and other smaller factions. Experts of Mesoamerican history believe this political setting in Tres Zapotes became more evident during the Epi-Olmec period in the cities.

By 400 BCE, the glory of La Venta was eventually lost. At the same time, Tres Zapotes became the undisputed center of the Olmecs. The city started going through cultural changes and what we now know as the Epi-Olmec period. Tres Zapotes and many neighboring cities experienced cultural changes and advancement in a civilization like they had never experienced before, and it's all because of the influx and influence of the Olmec in their societies.

Compared to the advancement seen in the previous Olmec centers, the Epi-Olmec experienced a much cruder advancement in art and architectural requirements. However, it was the time when the calendar system advanced a great deal within the region. When compared to later development in ancient Mexico, it seems unrefined. For example, the Tres Zapotes area was known as the base for the script called *Isthmian*. This type of writing was found all over several monuments and artifacts, and it became even more evident that it was the basis of the Mayan writing system some centuries down the line.

Excavations at the Tres Zapotes site uncovered more than 160 mounds and platforms, and they were dated back to the epi-Olmec period of 400 BCE to 200 CE. These mounds were grouped and labeled into four:

- Group 1
- Group 2
- Group 3
- Nestle Group

Each mound was made up of ruling political setups, royalties, and temples. For example, Group 2, which happens to be the most massive of the four, is strategically located at the middle of the site, while others were about a mile away from the four Groups.

Mesoamerican historians have concluded that the setting could only mean that Epi-Olmec Tres Zapotes was broken down into four political arrangements: royalties and ruling families. These four royal families ruled over the other parts of the cities in a decentralized system of governing.

It was also noted that the Epi-Olmec period was when there was little to zero flow of artifacts into the city, which was a sign that trade networks previously enjoyed at San Lorenzo and La Venta had collapsed. This was evident in the lack of finesse seen in the monuments, arts, pottery, and other architectural structures like what was obtainable during the original Olmecs. A further example can be seen in the type of basalt used by the Epi-Olmecs; it was more of inferior quality and must have made carving difficult. It could also be that the people lacked experienced craftsmen like the Olmecs had because many artifacts reflected the lack of detail.

Archaeologists noticed that by the dawn of the Classical era, the Tres Zapotes were not wholly abandoned yet, but there had been a significant shift in the people's way of life and culture. By 100 to 200 CE, it was evident that the Mesoamerican region was experiencing yet another type of change. Tres Zapotes, which had initially been influenced by the Olmec culture and civilization and had been on the western part of the homeland that made Epi-Olmec transition easier, once again changed alliance. The once Epi-Olmec center had now become a part of a different culture from the southern edge known as the *Classic Veracruz Culture*, or what some called the Gulf Coast Classic Culture. There were a few cities that came up at this time, but Tres Zapotes stood tall.

Some of these changes that came with the cultural shift at Tres Zapotes included the resumption of long-distance trading with other region members. The closed economy was finally opening up again – as it had been in San Lorenzo and La Venta. Also worthy of note was that the Classic Veracruz Culture experienced a further widened gap between the elites and the lower class. The social hierarchy experience during the Epi-Olmec was narrowed down, and wealth was now more in the hands of fewer people than it was previously. Just like what it was under the Olmecs for 2000 years, power became a lot more centralized.

The demand for unique crafts also increased; importation of luxury items from distant trade partners also rose to a new height. Lastly, religion grew in intensity, with a more formal structure now taking shape. The need for the elites to establish power and control among the people led to religious and ritual activities reaching new heights in Tres Zapotes, and the Classic Veracruz had several ceremonies to show off this power and control. These involved human sacrifices.

Once again, the Mesoamerican ball game was quite popular during this period, and it served as bridging the gap between the elites and other categories in the culture.

Gradually, art was taking shape and becoming more refined and unique in Tres Zapotes. A good example was the discovery of strange-looking carved figurines and statues with wheels and smiling faces. The findings revealed that they could have only been made in the earlier ADs, at a time known as the *Totonac civilization*. Some of the unique patterns noticed by archaeologists are still being studied in order to be translated.

The Classic Maya and the city of Teotihuacan in the Mexican highlands were the other civilizations that existed simultaneously with the Classic Veracruz culture. Archaeological findings at the Tres Zapotes site revealed the role of these nearby cultures on Tres Zapotes, which could only have been through trade networks.

Interestingly, some centuries after the fall of Teotihuacan, the Classic Mayan civilization also experienced a decline. As if the same thing plagued it, Tres Zapotes followed suit by losing its shine and went into decline. By 900 CE, Tres Zapotes was abandoned entirely, and only a few settlers were left to survive through the century. And so, it was that the 2,000 plus years run of Tres Zapotes as the Epi-Olmec center came to an end. No cities in ancient Mexican history had ever been inhabited for that long.

To date, discoveries are still being made concerning the city of Tres Zapotes.

Conclusion

The Olmec civilization is not getting the attention it should – despite its role in Mesoamerica and possibly in the world. We have carefully taken you on a journey from the first settlement in the region to what we have in modern-day Central America.

We began our journey by tracing it from as far back as 8000 BCE, a period known as the Archaic period before the emergence of pottery. This was when humans relied more on wild animals for sustenance; a period when hunting was the main occupation of the people. This was also the time where the people were always on the move. They had no particular place they could call home. Their movement depended on several factors like climate change, the availability of wild animals, the status of their settlements, and many others.

For better understanding, we broke down the Archaic period into the following categories:

- Early Pre-Classic Period - 2000 to 1000 BCE
- Middle Pre-Classic - 1000 to 400 BCE
- Later/Terminal Pre-Classic Period - 100 to 250 BCE

Each of these periods is unique to the region because further developments took place in the people's lives and cultures. We started noticing some form of complexity in societies as the people started moving around within the region.

The early settlements show that people started transiting from hunting to farming, from travelers to temporary settlers, and eventually seasonal and permanent settlers. This period was unique in Mesoamerica because the people began showing more interest in farming, and the population started to expand and become even more complex.

We noticed how the people took shelter in various rock shelters across the region. An example of one of them is the El Gigante rock shelter. Other settlements took shape around coastal resources, which is again based on the resources available; remember, there and a move away from hunting into another form of feeding the population.

The more extended settlement later led to the need for more farmlands, which led to clearing the forest using various crude tools and farming methods. Notably, domestication started, and maize became the most valued farm produce in the region.

Artifacts found at several archaeological sites across the region revealed how the people managed themselves without metal resources. Stone tools were the predominant method used to achieve farming, hunting, and sculpturing.

Obsidian proved to be another invaluable resource for the Olmecs, playing a particular part in the people's lives by being used as a tool, objects in religious rituals, and later in trade.

We also took you on a ride around some important archaeological sites within the region while talking about their uniqueness, the artifacts found there, and what made them stand out. We discussed religion, the various gods they worshipped, and the relevance of some of their rituals.

Then we talked about the Olmec, how they were called the "people of the rubber nation," "the rubber people" - all because they were located at a primary source of rubber raw material. We dove into the controversy surrounding the Olmecs' origin, the different views expressed by several scholars, and the reasons behind their position. Some even later changed their original position to a newer version - thanks to new archeological discoveries!

However, one thing was clear and agreeable to all the scholars: the Olmecs were more advanced in civilization and general way of life than considered at first. We can thank them for many advances and contributions to our modern society, like writing and long-count calendars.

The Olmecs were predominantly farmers who relied on specific farm products like maize. They also developed a unique irrigation system that supplied water across the cities and made it possible for all-year-round farming. As seen in other parts of the region, the Obsidian played a unique role among the people alongside other luxury items from other parts of the region.

The Olmecs enjoyed trading with other parts of the region and beyond. Scholars have argued that these trade networks and relationships with other parts of the region were responsible for their peculiar advancement and the complex nature of their society.

The history of the Olmecs is incomplete without talking about the Colossal Heads. These were massive stones with human faces that had striking resemblances carved on them using only stone tools. Some of these stone heads weigh as much as 40 tons and stand taller than most humans when upright. You have to admire the expertise in carving these faces because it was not one face for all, but each stone head had different features. This master-crafting was also seen in other artifacts like pottery, idols, and other architectural monuments.

The Olmecs were the first to create a class among the people in lifestyles and living arrangements. The elites had separate quarters distinct from the lower classes. The elites controlled the lower classes with religion and created fear among them with human sacrifices. The royals were treated as gods, and their words were laws because it was assumed that the gods were speaking through them.

We also noticed how various Olmec centers started from San Lorenzo to La Venta and eventually Tres Zapotes. These cities attained great prominence with unique developments before they eventually fell, one after the other. Several reasons have been attributed to the fall of these great centers, but they are all mere suggestions; no concrete conclusion has been arrived at. This is also because the Olmec civilization itself is based on archaeological findings and not on texts.

La Venta was the other Olmec center that came to the limelight after the fall of San Lorenzo and was occupied for about 500-years; it was a much more complex society, with class separation into royals, elites, and the low class. The inequality in wealth and other social standing widened further. Some luxury items were meant only for the elite. The priests were treated as having control over life and death and even wielded some political powers. We also noticed how the economy of La Venta thrived based on its strategic location and the ecosystems nearby. While San Lorenzo was known for its Colossal Heads and other monuments, La Venta was known for its complexes, plazas, and platforms.

The Olmecs had good trading relationships with neighboring civilizations like the Mayans and the Aztecs; they also dominated a few cities. This was evident in Epi-Olmec Tres Zapotes, where the cities were not wholly an Olmec center. Still, some versions of Olmec civilization and culture were practiced among the people for many years. Some scholars had even said that the presence of the Olmecs in Tres Zapotes (and everything they brought along when they abandoned La Venta) was the reason why Tres Zapotes became the regions where cities were most inhabited – lasting more than 2000 years!

Tres Zapotec, as Epi-Olmec center, initially closed its borders and did not transact business with other parts of the region until it underwent another transition that changed everything, and business resumed again with neighbors and faraway partners.

We cannot forget the role the Mesoamerican ball game played among the Olmecs. During the high of San Lorenzo as the Olmec center, we saw how the ball game was used among different political entities to serve different purposes. For some, it was mere entertainment that fostered unity, especially among the elites and the lower classes. For others, the sport had far-reaching consequences like losing your limps and even being sacrificed! This ball game is still in existence today and is the oldest ball game in the world.

The writing system found at the Olmec sites is the oldest in the region and possibly globally; it is still being translated. The Mayans' writing system and long-count calendars – initially thought to be the oldest and most advanced – have been correctly traced to the Olmecs.

You might call the Olmecs the oldest civilization in the Americas, and some might call them the *forgotten civilization*. However, history will not forget the role the Olmecs played in the history of the human race in general – and in the Americas specifically.

Here's another book by Enthralling History that you might like

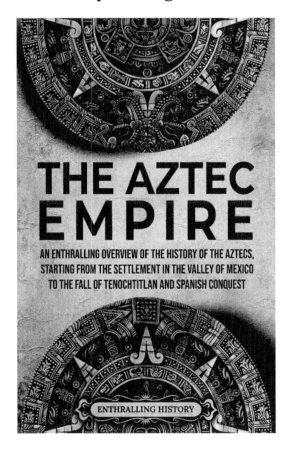

Free limited time bonus

Stop for a moment. We have a free bonus set up for you. The problem is this: we forget 90% of everything that we read after 7 days. Crazy fact, right? Here's the solution: we've created a printable, 1-page pdf summary for this book that you're reading now. All you have to do to get your free pdf summary is to go to the following website: **https://livetolearn.lpages.co/enthrallinghistory/**

Once you do, it will be intuitive. Enjoy, and thank you!

Bibliography

Richard A. Diehl. *The Olmecs: America's First Civilization (Ancient Peoples and Places)*. London: Thames & Hudson; November 1, 2005.

Michael D. Coe. Rex Koontz. *Mexico: From the Olmecs to the Aztecs (Ancient Peoples and Places)*. London and New York: Thames & Hudson; June 14, 2013.

Christopher A Pool. *Olmec archaeology and early Mesoamerica*. Cambridge and New York: Cambridge University Press, 2007.

Deborah L. Nichols. Christopher A. Pool. *The Oxford Handbook of Mesoamerican Archaeology*. Oxford University Press; September 24, 2012.

Douglas J. Kennett. *Archaic-Period Foragers and Farmers in Mesoamerica*. Sep 2012.

Rosemary A. Joyce. John S. Henderson. *Beginnings of Village Life in Eastern Mesoamerica*. Cambridge University Press; 20 January 2017.

Michael D. Coe. *Magnetic Exploration of the Olmec Civilization*. Yale University. January 1972(PDF online reproduction).

Karl A Taube. *Olmec Art*. Washington, D.C: Dumbarton Oaks Research Library and Collection; 2004.

Kathleen Berrin. (editor) Virginia M. Fields(editor). *Olmec: Colossal Masterworks of Ancient Mexico*. Yale University Press; October 26, 2010.

Mary Ellen Miller. *The Art of Mesoamerica (World of Art)*. Thames & Hudson; September 10, 2012.

Christopher A. Pool(editor). *Settlement Archaeology and Political Economy at Tres Zapotes, Veracruz, Mexico (Monographs)*. The Cotsen Institute of Archaeology Press; July 1, 2003.